Senior Online Dating

Dr. Martin Dorenbush

ISBN-10: 1482051761
EAN-13: 9781482051766
Library of Congress Control Number: 2013901417
CreateSpace Independent Publishing Platform
North Charleston, South Carolina

Senior Online Dating

Dr. Martin Dorenbush

CHAPTER ONE:

In the Beginning...

A fter an enchanted marriage of over forty-one years, the majority transcendent and the last few devastating, my wife finally succumbed to colon cancer after a fourteen-year battle, complete with multiple surgeries, courses of chemotherapy, and debilitating radiation treatment.

We had met almost fifty years ago at a hospital in New York, where I was a young intern and she was an emergency room nurse. She was Roman Catholic and I was Jewish, which made our relationship complicated. At that time, interfaith marriage was a rarity. Despite the negative reactions of our parents, friends, and other family members, we married. We were young, in love, and rightly felt that we could conquer all difficulties. In retrospect, we did.

After my wife died, I entered a long and difficult period of grief; my depression and despondency seemed overwhelming. My three children were now grown, had lives of their own, and were scattered about the country. Now the sole resident of a large, four-bedroom house, I gradually found myself living in the basement.

I managed to fill the endless days with computer surfing, reading, and long bicycle treks by myself. Lacking much interest in anything else, I went to bed each night with the fervent hope that I would not awaken in the morning. This state of affairs lasted almost three years. I did finally have the insight, however, that this torpor and chronic depression in which I had wrapped myself would have to end.

I had retired from the practice of ophthalmology about ten years previously, because I had developed a degenerative retinal condition. The surgical and laser procedures that comprise an active ophthalmologic practice require precise, acute, three-dimensional vision. Since I could no longer see well, I went from physician to caregiver of my spouse.

I did appreciate God's fine sense of humor. The affliction of an ophthalmologist with an eye disease was quite clever. I also realized that I should not complain too much; had I been a neurosurgeon, I would have undoubtedly developed a brain tumor.

After my wife's death, the increasing costs of maintaining the old house and my lack of income finally shook me out of my hermit-like existence. It was time to get on with life and establish a new reality. I now realized that my wife, Pat, would have been aghast at the way I had been behaving for the past three years. I was tired of living alone and taking meals alone. I craved human contact.

Friends and relatives who had watched with alarm how I was handling grief and mourning encouraged me to put the house on the market. They suggested that I relocate from the suburbs to a neighboring town, where I would have the opportunity to socialize and perhaps make new friends. Although the real estate market was depressed in my area, by sheer good luck, the house sold at a fair price.

I congratulated myself on having made a momentous decision. This structure that had been my home for over forty years was now just a simple piece of real estate. While every room contained memories of the past, these memories were now part of me and would remain with me forever, even when I would be living elsewhere.

Closing day was fast approaching, and I still had to find another place to live. An apartment in a neighboring town was the obvious solution. While I had not lived in an apartment for over fifty years, I was confident that I could cope. My chief difficulty was the inability to drive because of my vision, but living in the center of town would enable me to walk wherever I needed to go.

Loneliness is the chief problem for those of us who have lost a spouse through death or divorce. Our married friends gradually drift away. In a world that seems to be made for couples, we feel like we do not fit in very well. For widows and widowers, friends who knew us when we were all young are reminded of their own mortality when they see us, and they feel uncomfortable with us. We are, therefore, forced to make new friends and to forge new relationships.

I realized that I had not dated or socialized with women in over forty years. I did not know where to meet women, how to court women, and how someone in my age group should relate with women. In short, I did not know the rules of engagement. While still physically and mentally active, at least in my own opinion, I now thought about some new questions. What was I looking for? What was the endgame or goal of any new relationship with a woman?

During my high school and college years, these were simple questions to answer. Among my friends in their teenage years and early twenties, the goal of any date was to have a great time while also (and I mean no offense here) to achieve the impossible dream of getting laid. Now I wondered, was this to be the obvious goal at this later stage of my life?

What did I want a relationship to provide? The answer came easily. I wanted companionship—someone with whom to have dinner, go to a movie or concert, or enjoy a pleasant conversation. Most of all, I wanted to feel that I was not alone; I wanted the humanizing effect of another of my species close by. Mind you, the goal of my earlier years had not completely evaporated.

My sister and brother-in-law suggested that I look into on-line dating. Although I knew that such websites existed, I always thought they catered to younger people who found it difficult to socialize because of job constraints or lack of time due to hectic lifestyles. I never thought that these sites would be of any help to people in my age group.

As an apartment-warming present, my sister purchased a one-month membership for me in an online dating service. All I had to do was log on, complete a biography for the database, and I would soon enter the cyberworld of online dating. Suddenly I realized that I had a lot to learn.

CHAPTER TWO:

The Rules and Strategy of Engagement

Most online dating services appear to follow a similar pattern. They consist of vast databases of people who have expressed a desire to meet others for social and romantic reasons. The databases constantly expand as new members join the different services.

These sites request members to submit photographs and detailed biographical material when they enroll. Members complete a detailed questionnaire, providing answers in essay form to several incisive questions. Matches are made using sophisticated computer technology, providing enormous exposure to others in the database. Modern computer technology makes this exposure possible. The ultimate goal of marriage, if so desired by the member, appears to occur quite frequently, although I have no statistics to support this. I do know of three couples that met on computer dating sites and are now happily married.

Most online dating sites appear to have an international clientele, although the majority of members reside in the United States. An initial fee of about $39 per month, renewable for various time periods, is required. The major sites welcome all ages and religions, as long as the applicant pays the fee and submits the necessary information.

One large site has a marked Jewish flavor, with dating advice provided by rabbis, social directors, and authors of books dealing with Jewish themes. The site is appealing to non-Jews as well, however, because it is entertaining and full of relevant hints on how to conduct oneself in the chess game of finding a mate. This site's membership appears to be huge, most probably in the hundreds of thousands; it comprises all age groups and degrees of religious affiliation.

While dating sites may not lead to a permanent relationship, they certainly provide hours of banter, flirting, and interesting experiences. One begins by stating that he or she is a woman looking for a man or a man looking for a woman. I am not certain if there are other choices, but sites that cater to gay men and women are plentiful.

The next items covered are geographical location, age range desired, and what the member is seeking in a relationship. Is it marriage? A companion? A long-term relationship? Is it a date or something known as an *activity partner*? (I am not quite sure what this means.)

I found it interesting to read that about 25 percent of online dating service memberships are purchased as gifts by the parents of unmarried children. Perhaps children of unmarried parents purchase an equal number of memberships!

Various sites ask prospective members about their degree of religious affiliation, annual income, political position, and dietary habits. Members are expected to state how many children they have, if they currently live with them, and whether or not they wish to have more children. The websites ask for height, weight, hair and eye color, and of course zodiac sign. Subsequent questions ask food preferences, languages spoken, religious service attendance, and if converting to a different religion would be considered, as well as scores of other questions too numerous to list.

A list of favorite activities is appended to the sites. The most incisive areas appear to be the initial biography and shorter essays addressing what members are looking for in a match, and what physical and mental attributes ideal dates or partners should possess.

I will, however, note that there appears to be a great deal of innocent and perhaps not-so-innocent fabrication and writers' hyperbole. For example, there is often an obvious disconnect between a person's stated age and the submitted photograph. I also found it difficult to believe that sedentary folks, approximately age sixty, are truly mountain climbers, hang gliders and sky jumpers. All this, however, makes for a good mix, so reading through some of the submissions can be both entertaining and, at times, a bit sad. The databases for each gender appear to be huge, and the computer programs seem to work well at sending profiles of members to other members in the correct demographic and geographic area.

Upon logging onto an online dating site, there appears a possibly interesting list of people in one's area, requested age group, and gender. In my case, I receive about a dozen members' bios and photos per day. One is then expected to look at the photo, read the bio, and consider the answers to the numerous questions. A click box appears at each person's submission. Click a heart icon ("yes") and it becomes two hearts; click "no" and that particular member's information is deleted and will not be forwarded to your online dating site e-mail list again. A "maybe" click will bring that member's name back to you at some future time.

7

The main action, however, involves a yes click. When this is done, the member whose name you clicked gets an immediate e-mail announcing that another member has clicked yes. Now that person has access to your bio and information and is given the opportunity to click yes, no, or maybe. Should the member click yes, firecrackers, whistles, and bells seem to go off in cyberspace. Both of you receive an immediate e-mail stating that someone is interested in you and has clicked your name, and you are strongly encouraged to e-mail each other and start the ball rolling.

At this point, members remain totally anonymous. Both members have used screen names; there is no listing of addresses or telephone numbers, and any revelation of personal information depends on the progression and development of the e-mails between the members. There is, however, constant goading by the online dating staff to follow through, how to act, and what to write in the initial communications between members. This tends to come across as a kindly old matchmaker in cyberspace who knows everyone in the village and has already found out what the parents are ready to contribute tangibly and intangibly to secure a contract.

In summary, the concept of online dating is technologically brilliant. It provides people seeking to meet a significant other enormous exposure to potential mates; members are provided with minimal personal data concerning the future *match*; and early anonymity provides some measure of protection for the real possibility of having to kiss that dreadful frog.

These sites do, however, have one negative effect. In a sense, dating sites result in the curtailing of social interaction among men and women who are seeking compatible members of the opposite sex and may be searching for deeper emotional involvement with a potential partner.

Prior to online dating, people usually met at work, school, dances, fundraisers, and numerous other social events. Folks encountered each other, liaisons were made, and the normal course of male/female interaction took place. A certain percentage of these chance meetings resulted in the final goal of marriage. Now, with the advent of technologically enhanced dating, this no longer exists.

Members sit in front of a computer screen, read bios, evaluate photos, and try to determine the deepest feelings of other members who may or may not be truthful. The invaluable phase of meeting face-to-face, the spontaneity of the give and take of conversation, and the subtle clues of body language are delayed until the final meeting of members. At this point, the meeting members are probably apprehensive; they are on their guard and concerned about what is in store for them. The meeting may be quite positive or, likewise, quite negative.

With normal non-online dating, one has previously met the future date in a social setting and has already garnered much information and insight into how the date will progress. There is far less chance for fabrication and much less anxiety concerning the entire dating scenario.

Another negative associated with this online dating world is the curtailment of social interaction that does not deal with the romantic goals of the participants. Volunteer work, fundraising, and charitable work tend to lose valuable participants because those who seek to socialize in quest of possible romantic involvement with the opposite sex see no reason to take part in these activities.

It is far easier to sit in front of a monitor and simply click. One also tends to lose the social skills that are honed when men and women meet. Normal verbal and social interplay is a powerful aphrodisiac. In summary, I will mention that the sex attractant powers of male and female pheromones are lost online. Perhaps in the future, when computer technology reaches the level where scents can be downloaded as well as audio and video databases of online dating services' members, an important new parameter of a potential mate can be inhaled.

CHAPTER THREE:

Damn the Torpedoes, Full Speed Ahead

T he time for action had arrived. I turned to my worldly sister for advice about how to phrase my biography and enter certain crucial data. First of all, I was advised that fabrication and writer's privilege were integral parts of the online dating experience. These are among the cardinal rules to be followed:

1. *Never* reveal your true age. A listed age of over seventy is the kiss of death, and no one will ever bother with you.

2. Your photo may be current, but it must be carefully done. You must not use passport photos or cut-and-paste head-shots. It is best to seek out a local photographer who really knows how to use computer software to wipe out the majority of wrinkles, bags, and deep creases. I was told I was lucky, because I still had a relatively full head of hair. Beards and mustaches are undesirable.

3. Your height is *never* below five feet six inches, no matter how short you may be. Weight for a man is not too important, as it is not visible in the photo.

4. Enter *all* of the relationship categories listed, as you will take anything.

Prior to the final submission, my sister suggested that I first send her a copy, as I had no experience or talent for this arcane endeavor.

Before I knew what had happened, I was ready to upload my information to the database. Soon thousands upon thousands of women would be scrutinizing my photograph and reading my emotionally revealing essays and answers, both relevant and idiotic, that I gave to questions.

Ensconced in my new apartment, I had a paid-for one-month subscription to an online dating service. I had posted a suitable photograph and biography; yet I was still dealing with some emotional misgivings.

Was I—a confirmed member of the "golden years" demographic, a Social Security person who still remembered "creamsicles" and "more doctors smoke Lucky Strike than any other cigarette"—ready to join the quest for a new female relationship? I was the survivor of an enchanted marriage of more than forty years, and a long-term resident of what I considered *Camelot*, who now occupied a one-bedroom apartment in a nondescript New Jersey town.

I well remember the difficulties my future wife and I had in coming to grips with the question of whether we should marry. This potential union was severely frowned upon by the church, as well as by both sets of parents. Our close friends could only be described as uncertain and slightly dismayed at our subsequent decision.

In the end, it took a war to goad us into a decision. The conflict in Vietnam was raging; I had received orders requiring me to report to the Second Marine Division at Camp Lejeune, North Carolina. I was now a fully trained ophthalmologist, and there was a billet awaiting me at the Naval Hospital, Danang. American casualties were rising, and the future was uncertain.

We were married the week before I was due to report. For the next forty-one years, through times that were transcendent in happiness until the end, when the horror of rapidly progressing metastatic cancer ensued, our marriage flowered.

Was it now possible or even proper for me to seek a relationship with another? Was this an unfaithful strike at the memory of my Pat, as well as a selfish and dishonorable act?

The answer to this agonizing question began about a year after Pat died. While attempting to deal with the catastrophic mental trauma and depression produced by her death, I joined and finally became a moderator of an online bereavement site. Grieving members of the site would post messages describing our feelings and emotional difficulties; the rest of the members would, as best they could, try to give emotional support in response to the posts.

I remember very well the post I received from one member, a gentleman my age whose wife had died fairly close to the time of my Pat. He announced in a joyous posting that he had met another woman, a member of the same site. They had enjoyed vigorous online chats, multiple extended telephone calls, and finally several weekends together. Both felt that they had a great deal in common and could best help each other by union. I could not believe what I had read and telephoned my friend, asking him to explain to me how this impossible act could take place.

I paraphrase the conversation:

"Marty, I am not as well educated or as able as you are to put into words what I feel. I will try to answer your question as best I can. I cannot ever forget the wonderful life I had with my wife. This will stay with me forever, and she is always in my heart. My wife would never have wanted me to suffer grief for the rest of my life if there was some chance for happiness. While we were married, we always tried to do things to make each other happy—gifts, kind words, surprises, kisses and caresses—without number. Why should this stop just because one of us is now absent? I have a large, roomy heart, and my wife has simply moved over a bit to make room for the woman who will lift me from this terrible state of loss and loneliness to a state where I may be happy again."

I listened carefully and wished him and his new love the best of fortune, but I had my doubts. It took me an additional eighteen months to realize the profundity of this action and explanation. My Pat would also be aghast at the way I had behaved during the past two and a half years. The unremitting unhappiness that her death produced was not her fault. I was dishonoring her by wallowing in self-pity.

I came to understand that our species is capable of unlimited amounts of love. Should I be fortunate enough to establish a deep relationship with another woman, I realized that I was capable of loving again.

But once more, unresolved questions began to swirl about me.

Were not people in my age group more or less fixed in our ways, suspicious of strangers, intolerant of change, and—most of all—not as attractive as we once were? Would my children think of me as a foolish old man whose judgment was impaired? Literature is replete with novels, plays, and operas detailing the foibles of elderly gentlemen seeking love and romance.

More perceived difficulties began to arise. What if I met someone and we decided to live together? Who would move in with whom? Would I have to break my apartment lease if I turned out to be the one who must move? Would I be expected to take any future relationship to the highest level, i.e., marriage? The thought of a wedding reception with orchestra, dinner, flowers, and all the other paraphernalia seemed ridiculous.

Did one save or spend more if a joint relationship ensued? If a marriage did occur, would children on both sides worry about their potential inheritances? What was all that stuff I had read about prenuptial contracts?

A terrible thought entered my confused mind. Would this strange woman I would be living with want to see me naked? Like all men my age, I had some flab; I had lost muscle tone in many areas. I had skinny legs, wrinkles, and all the other physiologic changes of aging. Even worse, I realized with horror, was that I would also be expected to view this woman of a certain age in *her* naked state. But then I had one positive thought: At least in our age group, there would most likely be early senile cataract formation, with some loss of visual acuity. Perhaps in dim light, both of us in our unclothed state would not look too bad.

"Enough," I reasoned. All of these worries were premature. The odds of any woman desiring to see me naked were miniscule. If I did meet someone, I would be fully clothed, as would she—at least for the initial first few dates.

A more serious scenario began to present itself. Suppose all went well with dating and such. Suppose I had met a most compatible woman, we were now living together, and deeper feelings had started to develop in both of us. We would both be at the age when physical decline starts and serious illnesses, some of which are terminal, occur. Would she or I be able to just walk away and leave the other? Was this the expected action if one partner became ill and no marriage had taken place?

To put it in a more personal light: was I ready to be a caregiver again? I did not think that I had the physical, emotional, or financial abilities to do so. If the situation were reversed, could I expect any woman I met to do the same for me? Any woman who would be interested in me would probably be in the same age group as I was. Neither of us would be starry-eyed youngsters who would easily repeat the words, "in sickness or in health, 'til death us do part." Would either of us just gloss over the potential perils? In the end, I had no answers to these questions swirling about me. I was simply a member of an online dating site, of sound mind (I hoped), and would proceed.

Probably worst of all were the never-ending television ads for Viagra, Levitra, and others. Would I ever need these? Better yet, would I ever have the occasion to need these? I could go no further at this point. I needed to do some serious thinking. I would have to seek help in order to cope with these self-generated daunting problems.

I decided that I needed further input in order to make what I considered now to be quite a momentous decision. Where else to go, but online? I contacted a woman, a member of a bereavement site I had moderated during that first dreadful year of mourning. She ran a singles social site and appeared to be quite savvy in the area of online dating. She listened patiently to what I was contemplating and was not too sanguine about the entire endeavor.

She pointed out the numerous potential problems that could arise. Aside from well-meaning people seeking companionship, there were others out there who could present situations I had never even considered.

I learned that there were predators out there—not only financial predators (bad enough) but emotional predators (even more dangerous). I learned that there were people who, through no fault of their own, were mentally and emotionally stressed. Like people drowning, they would cling to and eventually drown anyone attempting to establish a romantic liaison with them.

She told me I was a "babe in the woods," emotionally naive, because I had not tried to establish a new relationship with a woman in over forty years. Because I was fragile and not fully in charge of my emotions, she felt that I was unable to make social decisions after such a devastating catastrophe of spousal loss. She asked me to promise that I would let her first vet any woman I met before the relationship became too deep. A review would be made of all the correspondence, and I was also to keep notes about any telephone conversations I had.

I listened in amazement to this litany of dire perils of quicksand, alligators, poisonous pigmy blowgun darts, armies of ants, and thirty-foot anaconda snakes that swallow goats. Did I really want to go on this safari? Was I up to being a Henry Stanley in search of my Dr. Livingston?

I pulled myself together and gently told her that after almost fifty years of medical practice that involved interviewing and in-depth meetings with probably hundreds of thousands of patients, I was well-versed in recognizing any such overt emotional behavior. This only appeared to confirm her opinion of my social skills. I did promise to keep her informed, but I said that I was a big boy now and could take care of myself.

CHAPTER FOUR:

A Bite of Reality Sandwich

During the four weeks prior to becoming a dating service member, I had moved into a one-bedroom apartment in a six-story high rise. I thought that this would be ideal for me, since the large volume of tenants would surely include a sizeable number of eligible women in my age group.

I quickly became friends with the doorman, George, who informed me that the building was overrun with eligible widows who would be excited to learn that a single man had moved in. Things began to look up.

Within a week, George invited me to meet him in the lobby for a "serious talk." He knew of a comely woman in the building who provided live-in care for an elderly couple. She was most pleasant, a good cook, attractive for her age, but devout and a minister in her church. I had previously told him that I was a "non-denominational bachelor" who was open to all potential liaisons. He assured me that I would not be dragged to church and that this woman was "a find."

During this conversation, I heard the elevator door open, and George said, "Here she comes now." I was totally unprepared. Surely this was one of the most terrible jungle perils that my online dating consultant had warned me about.

A pleasant woman of about thirty approached us, and George introduced me to her as "the new boy in town." I shook hands with this pretty lady, who inquired why I had moved into the building. She seemed so warm and friendly that I immediately lapsed into my narrative of how my wife had recently passed away and talked about the ordeals of mourning.

She listened sympathetically and then asked if the Lord had been helpful in my recovery. I gently explained to her that I was not a religious person; I was not even of her faith, but I certainly respected her beliefs and thanked her for her kind words. I could see that this extreme piety and, even more, the age difference would not work. George rolled his eyes and assured me that the case was not yet closed.

The only other female I met during the first weeks was a pleasant, white-haired octogenarian who lived alone in the apartment opposite mine. Apparently, one evening when I had arrived home late, I had inadvertently left my keys in the lock. The following morning, there was a tap on my door. When I opened it, there was my neighbor, keys in hand. I was scolded in a kindly manner, advised about all the perpetrators lurking about the building, just looking for keys in locks. Unless I shaped up, it was clear that she thought I would not be around for long.

I quickly apologized for my miscreant behavior and promised to always make sure that my keys were not left in the lock. It did not take much reflection to determine that some outside help, such as an online dating site, was vital to my socialization plans.

Just prior to becoming a dating service member, I had to deal with the closing of my house. This went quite well, but after the realtor, lawyer, township, state, home equity loan bank, and multiple others took their cuts, I was left with a greatly diminished check. The closing took place in the morning, and after lunch I presented myself with check at the offices of Lucretia, the financial planner.

Lucretia was a no-nonsense, middle-aged Italian lady of ample proportions with a green eyeshade.

"Martin," she said, "I see my job as trying to make the funds you received from the sale of your home last for the rest of your life. According to insurance statistical tables, you have about ten years left to live."

"Only ten!" I croaked.

"Not to worry," she said. "It's only a statistical estimate. You could get hit by a bus tomorrow."

This bit of information cheered me up, and she continued, "You must tell me how much money you need per month to live in the style you want. Since you are single, live in a one-bedroom apartment, do not drive, and have no one else to support, that figure should not be a large amount."

I thought for a moment and then said, "Three thousand dollars per month in addition to my social security."

My statement was met with silence. Lucretia looked at me with a gimlet eye through the green eyeshade. I waited, and then blurted out, "Two thousand five hundred per month." Still no reply. Only a hard look.

"Two thousand per month?" She smiled and snapped her fingers. The office door opened, and a minion entered with espresso and biscotti. It suddenly struck me that I had witnessed this scene before in *The Godfather,* where the budding Don Corleone discusses with a landlord whether or not an elderly tenant friend of the Don's wife can keep a dog in her apartment.

We shook hands on the deal, although at first I thought we would cut our thumbs, mingle blood, and a picture of a saint would be burned in my palm.

Lucretia said, "We will have to do about six percent. It's difficult, but doable. In an extreme case we might have to invade principal, but in your age group (I could practically hear her thinking *read old)* this is acceptable. There must be no frivolity—no fast cars or fancy women!"

I hastily assured her that this would never happen. "I am," I told her, "a sedate, retired physician." I said I led a solitary life, did not run with women, and would clean my plate at every frugal meal.

I stood up, kissed her ring, and backed out of the conference room. I could not wait to receive my first allowance check.

CHAPTER FIVE:

Lessons from Madison Avenue

B efore actually corresponding with and calling members with whom one is interested in potentially forming a relationship, careful attention must be paid to the completion of your own database.

The most important part of the online database appears to be the biographical essay. In this portion of the application, members are asked to provide *in essay form*, a rather lengthy description of themselves. Applicants should concentrate on positive factors and explain what they hope to achieve as members of the online dating service. This essay comprises the initial part of the posted information concerning new members. The staff members at most of these sites advise members to be truthful, upbeat, and light-hearted, and to try to convey a positive picture of themselves and what they are seeking in potential matches.

Most of the bios I read were from female members that had been referred to me as potential matches. Many of the biographies seemed narcissistic and boring. I do admit that it is difficult to emphasize one's positive attributes without seeming somewhat self-aggrandizing. However, the majority of members tended to be excessively self-complimentary. Because many of these initial essays had definite similarities, I found them quite repetitive and dull.

Practically all of the members listed the same activities and "likes." It appeared that all the submitters enjoyed long walks, short walks, beach time, and time in the mountains. Especially common was what I call the "universal trio." This included time spent with family—especially grandchildren—playing golf, and playing bridge. I admit that these are all noble and uplifting activities, but they do not rank high on what the male members of the dating service are seeking in a potential liaison.

It is important when composing the biographical essay to understand its function. This is the portion of the database first presented to the opposite sex. If the essay is excessively narcissistic and boring and includes the *terrible trio* mentioned above, it will probably fail to attract potential dates.

Before the biographical essay is posted, carefully consider its purpose. Basically, the essay is advertising copy. Try not to consider writing the essay as a homework assignment in Creative Writing 101. Your words should be light-hearted, sparkling in nature, and attractive to members of the opposite sex. As crude and perhaps as demeaning as it sounds, you are marketing *yourself* as a manufacturer would a new shampoo or a new automobile. The bio must be written to appeal to members of the opposite sex in the age group you are interested in. An essay written by a thirty-year-old woman intended to appeal to thirty- and forty-year-old men will differ radically from that written by a sixty-year-old woman seeking to meet sixty- and seventy-year-old men.

You must, as much as possible, try to distinguish yourself from the thousands of other writers who are trying to catch the eye of the same members in the targeted demographic. Complete the essay skillfully, perhaps with a bit of humor, and a moderate amount of hyperbole and "writer's privilege."

As an example: In an ordinary, boring biographical essay, the writer may describe herself as a sixty-something, attractive grandmother. This description will immediately conjure up in the seeking male's mind a motherly, wrinkled, kindly old woman of short stature with dyed blue/silver hair. This is not a positive, vibrant, sexual image to present to a fit sixty-year-old male who seeks a female partner probably younger than he is. He desires to meet a woman who is full of life and still interested in the intimacy that probably all of the male members consider most important in any relationship that may deepen and progress.

The woman mentioned in the above example would better attract male members' attention if she instead described herself as "a vibrant, voluptuous woman who, although now a grandmother, has not lost any vitality." She could write, "An attractive, caring female is currently seeking a relationship with a similarly vibrant and caring male who can appreciate her as the vigorous and young-in-heart-and-body woman that she is."

Forget the hiking, biking, walking, movies, opera, and pop music that most, if not all, of the competition will list. You must be different. The activities and things you enjoy doing must appeal to the correct age and male demographic to which you are "making your pitch."

If this sounds crass, so be it. Just remember why you have sent in forty bucks and probably much more to have the opportunity to post your product on the online dating site. The *product,* my dear reader, is *you.*

I now speak to women seeking men: You may feel some-what uncomfortable speaking about it, but probably number one or two on a typical male online dating site member's list of attributes desired in a female member is the opportunity to establish a relationship in which intimacy will play a promi-nent role. By no means am I encouraging female members to appear promiscuous or wanton in the biographical essay. But certain code words in your biography will distinguish you from other female site members. You want to be perceived as a "loving, romantic, affectionate, caring, and warm woman" with a marked interest in all things relevant to male-female relationships.

Ladies, you know exactly what I mean. You have been us-ing these tactics all of your lives; just because you now find yourself a member of an online dating site is no reason to abandon them. We guys love this stuff and respond to it.

Men also love to see evidence in a bio that a woman can cook gourmet meals, enjoys watching sporting events, and will do her best to make her future man happy because she knows he will do his best to make *her* happy. Most of us re-ally do not like to play golf with our women; we do not like to play bridge with our women; and a significant percentage of us are not avid opera aficionados. For God's sake, leave these out of your bios.

A word about the submitted photographs: Most people pay particular attention to the photographs of potential dates. Un-fortunately, the vast majority of these photographs are drab. People often submit unflattering photographs, which, for the most part, do not provide a positive impulse for other members to begin a potential relationship.

The worst photographs I have seen portray women with disheveled hair and frumpy clothing. Other unattractive photos have arms and legs cropped off. Equally off-putting are members who pose with various animals, grandchildren or, even more bizarre, with their previous spouses. No rocket science is involved here. Seek out a local photographer who is familiar can use computer software to enhance the image.

Before any photographs are taken, visit your hairstylist or barber and make sure your clothing is neat, attractive, and up-to-date. I would suggest no beards or mustaches for men. Women, make sure your makeup is attractive. Try to achieve a smile, but don't show too many teeth. Try to achieve a twinkle in your eyes that portrays an intimation of deeper things to come. Studying photographs of celebrities can provide more insight into creating an attractive photograph.

In summary, writing an effective biographical essay is not rocket science. It is simply describing what you have been doing for the past fifty or sixty years. However, because of the recent technological advances of online dating, you must now put actions into the form of words.

CHAPTER SIX:

The Truth and Nothing but the Truth

S ometimes when we attempt to present ourselves to others, especially as objects of desire, we may employ certain tactics that will tend to hide or somewhat ameliorate our perceived shortcomings.

For example, a little Botox here, a nip and tuck there, the combing of a few eight-inch long scalp hairs over a square area of half the skull, a bit of silicon strategically placed, a lip or two made fuller, or perhaps some ridiculously priced implants of various types superiorly and inferiorly situated on the body. These techniques certainly play a large part—as well they should—in the online dating game of life. They are all harmless; they really involve no deceit and are certainly part of the human experience.

One aid, however, presents danger if used. I refer to stretching the truth, which may range from author's privilege to frank fabrication. When I first came to online dating, I imagined that a bit of hyperbole and some fabrication were integral parts of the experience. But the women I met told me that they were very upset when they found out that men they met online had deceived them or lied to them. Most of the fabrications these women were discontented with related to the photograph, purported age, height, level of education, amount of income, and prime reason for becoming a member of an online dating service (read *sex*).

In the majority of cases, it did not take long for these savvy women to "smell a rat," and these nascent relationships were quickly terminated. Guys, I am not advocating the abandonment of attempts to come across as a more desirable male, but I would strongly advise not messing with the above parameters.

I found that these women really wanted an upfront kind of relationship. Any negative factors could be brought up gradually, as necessary, as a relationship deepened.

And now, *mea culpa, mea maxima culpa!* Part of my online database was kindly completed by my most knowledgeable sister. She was, and still is, of the firm opinion that age is important to female members of online dating sites. Her adage is "the younger, the better," so we need to "tweak" the number. I was, therefore, tweaked from seventy-three to sixty-eight. In my defense, though, I firmly believed, as do we all, that I really did not look my age. Age is just an irrelevant number, and so on. So, according to my profile, I was now a youthful male dater.

For the next couple of weeks, as I met and interacted with several women, my age was never an issue. Surely, I thought, I looked sixty-eight and probably even younger. I thought perhaps a little more tweaking would be helpful and soon looked into it. My denouement began innocently enough.

In order to add some spice to my bio, under the question asking "What languages do you speak?" Vietnamese was listed as one of the choices. Why not? I checked the box, knowing that this would make me stand out from those who were not speakers of Vietnamese. In reality, though, at one time I actually had a pretty sizable Vietnamese vocabulary. I was detailed to the Second Marine Division at Camp Lejuene, North Carolina, in the sixties during the war. I was about to be deployed to Naval Hospital, Danang, and was given courses in basic language skills. I learned about the delights of pungi sticks, spider holes, and all the other creative ways one could get killed while "in country." Alas, someone else volunteered for my billet, and I was never deployed. I did, however, speak a little Vietnamese; so including this on my info questionnaire did not rise to the level of mendacity.

Back to my fall from grace…I received a very pleasant e-mail from another online dating member, a woman in her early sixties. She had just finished reading my bio and came away with a question for me to answer. Like herself, I was raised in the Bronx. How did a nice Bronx boy come to speak Vietnam-ese? To her knowledge, there were no Viet Cong lurking in the wilds of the Grand Concourse!

We soon found ourselves at the next level, happily chatting on the telephone, discussing high schools and even the college we had both attended. We discussed the famous teenage hang-outs in the Bronx, the bus routes, the restaurants, and what we did as kids. The conversation was most spontaneous, and I threw caution to the wind. When asked what year I had graduated from college, it did not take me long to come up with the correct date.

At this point, I thought that I had heard some mental mouse clicks once I replied. Suddenly the tone and cadence of her voice dropped. I thought I now heard the occasional hiss and drop of venom.

"I see," she said. "You were graduated from college at the age of twelve."

I was lost—trapped by a savvy lawyer. I stammered, began to sweat, and became fearful that a cobra would strike deep in the ear that was pressed to the phone. The guru was right. It was not a goat-eating anaconda, but a wily, highly educated trial lawyer serpent got me. One chance existed. Perhaps I could "cop a plea" with this attorney.

I decided to try to use the Nuremburg Nazi Defense.

"Nicht schuldig, nicht schuldig," I moaned. "I plead *not guilty*. I was just following orders. My sister made me do it." This was followed by a long silence; then she asked the next question:

"How old are you really?"

"Seventy-three," I quickly answered.

"Not good enough," was the reply. "When will you be seventy-four?"

"In August," I quickly replied.

"Then you are closer to seventy-four, right?"

"Yes, yes, Your Honor," I managed to croak. Another very long silence. Could I be sued for "breach of biography" or perhaps even wire fraud, since computers and telephones were in play? I waited for the verdict.

"'Martin," my inquisitor said, with a bit less of a cobra tone, "I have considered this conversation. What you did was not only dishonest, but despicable."

"Yes, yes," I said with a pronounced cry of contrition.

"The one thing in your favor," said Torquemada, was that I had admitted my guilt, now was up-front with my age, and realized the error of my ways.

A potential relationship could be possible, but the Court and The Doctrine of the Protection of the Faith people would closely watch me.

It was a harsh sentence, but at least the fire could be extinguished. Needless to say, I looked forward to meeting Torquemada for dinner. I really did relish this type of verbal play.

But now I'm getting ahead of my story.

CHAPTER SEVEN:

The Battle Is Joined

My one-month membership had been paid, my photograph and corrected biographical essay were online, and most of the numerous questions concerning my innermost desires and idiosyncrasies were now in cyberspace.

The decision had been made. At 8:00 a.m. sharp, I arose from bed, put on my gear, and boarded the LST. The sea was choppy, the sky was gray, and the distant shores of the web lay ahead. No doubt I would soon encounter devastating enemy fire, mines, and viciously cutting razor-sharp wire—probably even goat-swallowing anacondas.

I fought my way to the computer. My hands trembled as I logged on, entered my password, and was now in contact with thousands of people. The ever-informative dating site computer informed me that at the moment over twenty thousand people were online with me.

I decided to follow only some of my infallible sister's rules of engagement. I had started to believe that since Old World matchmakers no longer existed and I was no longer in the age group for an arranged marriage, online dating was my best shot at what I hoped to achieve.

My answers to the short questions would, for the most part, not be fabrications. The essays and the short paragraphs needed to respond to the rather incisive questions concerning feelings, desires, and expectations would be explicit and truthful. I would attempt to describe in words to countless thousands of members my deepest and innermost thoughts and feelings.

After examining and pondering all of the various online dating staff advisories, what I came away with was the need for honesty. However, when I composed my first biography, I was so honest that I described the passing of my wife in too much detail. I wrote about how this devastating turn of events affected me and how I was now gasping for help. It did not require a degree in rocket science to see why replies to this dismal post were almost non-existent. After several days of website silence, I reread the bio and was appalled at what I had written.

My next biography, although not a fun-filled short story, was far more upbeat, with an occasional spark of quirky humor. Once it was submitted, the voice on my computer said, "You have mail," so often that I was forced to lower the volume.

I received a message with a list of members that had met my criteria of gender, age, and geography. I was advised to read their bios, study their photos, and try to learn all about them. I was also aware that my biography, photograph, and personal information were, in turn, being examined by unknown numbers of women who, also in turn, had listed criteria matching what I had to offer. As Holmes would have said, "The game was afoot."

I started to read through the assignment I had been given. So far, all of the members were female. Good. Many of them lived in the county in which I lived, although about half the number lived in New York City, which was out of my geographical request area. I guess a special exception is made for New Yorkers who are probably so cosmopolitan that they are welcome in adjoining areas.

The women were all within the correct age group, although there were a few women of fifty-plus, as well as some who were seventy-plus. I would imagine that there is a bit of age leeway, as many members appear to be unsure of their correct age. So far, so good, I decided.

After a time, the biographies began to become somewhat repetitious. Everyone appeared to be interested in hiking, biking, long walks in the park, short walks on the beach, cooking, eating, concerts, opera, movies, etc. Interestingly, there were a few sixty-year-plus old members who mountain climbed, sky dived and were hang gliders. Practically all of the members whose names were forwarded to me described the pleasure they derived from their grandchildren and the importance to them of close family ties.

However, reading carefully between the lines, I soon realized that most, if not all, the members were lonely. They had lost a large, important part of their lives as a result of spousal death or divorce. At times this loss was expressed openly, without apology, and with a determination to try to do something about it.

At the end of each member's entry in the database, the click boxes, (yes, no, maybe) appeared. Should one become totally smitten with the presented member, the online dating staff encouraged the viewer to skip over the click feature and directly e-mail the member. Suggestions were given as how to word this initial dating communication.

One was advised to be brief but complimentary; one could mention some item in the member's posting in a positive fashion, and then end with a friendly, upbeat phrase or two. For those who were too timid to post their own words, a Cyrano de Bergerac feature existed. One could simply send a pre-printed "flirt message," such as "You pique my interest," or "I am interested. Are you?" Once these messages were sent, the ball literally was in the opposite court.

I was still uncertain about the rules of engagement, so I chose a member and wrote, "Hi, you sound like a real interesting woman, and I really like your pretty photo. I would like to get to know you better." While not brilliant, I hoped this would be somewhat effective. Total exhaustion set in; an hour of cyber romance had worn me out.

After a troubled night's sleep, dreaming about what I had done, I could not wait to check my e-mail the next morning. There were four "alerts" awaiting me. I was ordered to log onto the dating site immediately, read these messages, and respond to them without delay. Was this to be the electronic fulfillment to all of my desires? Would the impossible dream really come true forty years later?

Most of the messages were short. All of them were complimentary. No quicksand or alligators here. I was deemed an interesting person, rather good looking, and certainly someone that the responder would like to get to know better. The choice of whether or not to move to the next level in this reality video game was mine.

During the four weeks after I became a member of one on-line dating service, the computer informed me that over three hundred women members had viewed my profile. I received over fifty e-mails; about twenty other women had flirted with me, sent cards to my e-mail address, or contacted me via instant messaging.

Here lies the unbelievable value of sites like this. The exposure one receives is local as well as national and international.

I have received communications (not all of them within the realm of normal) from Africa, Australia, Britain, and Israel. Nigeria appeared to be quite active, with several women proclaiming themselves to be deeply in love with my photograph and biography.

Reading through the dozen or so member profiles which I received daily proved to be fun, and, as I have mentioned previously, at times sad. The overwhelming feeling expressed in the biographies I read was that of loneliness. The ratio of divorced women to widows was about equal. There were also several women in their sixties who admitted to never having been married and were actively seeking companions.

I must admit that when I first became involved with online dating, I naively thought I should shy away from those women who admitted to being divorced. I was of the ridiculous notion that these women had demonstrated their inability to form a lasting relationship with a man. Even more importantly, I thought, they were carrying emotional baggage precipitated by a nasty breakup. This turned out to be foolishness on my part, and I soon abandoned that belief.

CHAPTER EIGHT:

The New Fountain of Youth

During my written, oral, and face-to-face encounters with female members, I began to realize how skittish the women were. These online meetings with strangers seemed to produce a significant amount of apprehension and anxiety for them, perhaps because sooner or later, they knew they would be forced to reveal some of their deepest and innermost thoughts and longings to a complete stranger.

Of course, they had tried their best to evaluate the men they met by reading their biographies, studying their pictures, and analyzing their e-mails. At rare times, some of them even used the telephone. These women were obviously familiar with the potential dangers. After all, had not a woman who met a bona fide medical student through Craigslist been strangled by him? The concept of homicidal crazies was enough; other men sought financial gain, some were sexual predators, and quite a number of younger men in their twenties and thirties sought older women as "sugar mamas."

At the other end of the spectrum were older men in poor health, who were seeking "a purse or a nurse," as some women said. Many of these women were so concerned with matters of maintaining security that they even refused to reveal their first names until significant communication had occurred. I certainly understood their fears; but I felt this fear did not apply to me, as a macho male.

Two movies, *Basic Instinct* and *Sliver*, did bring potential danger to my mind. But any possible risk seemed to add to the excitement of the chase, and I quickly discounted it. I made a mental note that should things progress to a significant bedroom scene, I would check my partner's handbag to make sure there was no ice pick inside.

Typing back and forth online with women became tedious. I wanted to move this process along in a more timely fashion. After all, none of us were getting any younger, and this back-and-forth game could go on forever.

It dawned on me that I felt like I had been transported back in time to my high school and college years. I now thought about dating, what one did on dating, what to wear, what lines to say, when to kiss, how to kiss, what to touch, what not to touch, and many other considerations I had not entertained for over forty years. This was therapeutic in a most fantastic way.

I felt young again! I had suddenly lost forty years. When I looked in the mirror, I appeared younger. Most of all, I *felt* younger, both mentally and physically. Had I found a fountain of youth in deepest New Jersey? My God, I was about to go out on dates with women again, like I did at the age of seventeen. I even *felt* like a seventeen-year-old, with the added advantage of not having to show an ID in order to drink. The down side, however, was that at seventeen, I could drive my old straight-eight Pontiac with the shade over the windshield. At this new seventeen, however, I had lost my license.

I also noticed that this sudden removal of scores of years applied to the women as well. They tended to write mushy drivel in their notes, they giggled a lot, and were more vibrant and full of life than a woman in her sixties should be. They were being asked out on dates! They needed new, youthful clothes; they would not color their hair silver ever again; they could wear low high heels instead of sensible orthopedic type shoes. Best of all, they could tell their incredulous children that they could not babysit grandchildren on certain evenings because they "had a date and were going out."

Children and grandchildren could not wait for grandma to get back and relate all that might or might not have happened. She could now act coy, smiling those secretive smiles that had not been used for such a long time.

Medically speaking, it is my belief that both sexes using online dating services receive a good shot of the essential teenage hormones that have been absent for a long time. Ridiculous notion? I believe not. There is surely a medical study here, waiting to be done.

CHAPTER NINE:

Preparing for the First Date

The initial telephone contact with a potential date is akin to two sumo wrestlers circling each other in the ring. It is clumsy, slow, lacking in spontaneity, and fraught with receiving a heavy mental slap or push from your opponent. After the incredible hard work of securing a telephone number from the potential online date, the sumo match begins.

In my experience, there have been several e-mail communications between us. These were all perfunctory, non-revealing, and, at times, of a most idiotic nature. Finally I managed to extract a phone number, most commonly a cell phone number. This was probably done because the female dating site member believed that the online homicidal maniac would have a harder time finding out where she lived if he didn't have a home phone number. Not so, my female readers.

The phone call began as follows:

Me: Hi, cuddles44. This is Marty from the dating service. (I usually had to work with some inane screen name until more familiarity became established.)
She: Who?

Me: Marty—Marty from the online dating outfit. We just sent each other e-mails about five minutes ago.

She: Oh, yes. Now I remember.

Me: *To myself: Great short-term memory retention.* I was really looking forward to this telephone conversation—*like looking forward to a root canal.* Your biography was ever so interesting and the picture of you is terrific. *Did I just feel my nose grow?*

She: I really liked reading about you, and you look so young and handsome in your picture.

Me: *Just you wait, baby.*

She: How long have you been on this dating service?

Me: Oh, I just joined about ten minutes ago. My sister really pushed me into it. *I am really not such a loser that I have to find dates through an online dating service.*

She: I have been on this service for a year or two.

Me: *In reality, probably two to four years.* I was really interested in your bio, especially the hiking, biking, short walks, long walks, beaches, mountains, operas, movies, reading, bridge, golf, and untold amounts of time visiting grandchildren. Really, these are all the things I love to do.

She: Then we really have a lot in common.

Me: We sure do. Gee, you sound so great on the phone; I can't wait to meet you.

She: Me too.

We both hear the sounds of several sumo slaps and grunts.

Me: I see you live pretty close by. Could you possibly tell me your first name, or are you really called cuddles44?

She (giggling): My name is Faith.

Me: *I like cuddles better.*

She: Let's do coffee.

Me: I really would like to go out for dinner. I can do coffee at home, but I rarely get to go out for a meal. *Nobody wants to go out with me.*

She: You really want to go out for dinner on the first date?

Me: Sure thing. You sound like so much fun! I really want to spend more time with you—not just over coffee.

She: *Have I got a weirdo here?* Can you suggest a place in a crowded, well-lit area with multiple exits? *At least give me a fighting chance to escape from the homicidal maniac.*

Me: Sure. How about the food court at the mall?

She: Perfect. What day?

Me: How about Monday?

She: I can't do Monday. How about Tuesday?

Me: Sure. What about eight o'clock?

She: I can't do eight. I like to eat early.

Me: *Oh, my God! I got hooked up with a senior citizen who goes for the 4:30 early-bird special.* How about seven?

She: Sounds good.

Me: Will I be able to recognize you from your picture?

She: The picture is a tiny bit old. I may have gained a bit of weight since it was taken.

Me: Don't worry. How could I miss such a fascinating woman?

She (giggling): See you soon. Marty.

I found that as time went by, telephone conversations became easier. A certain pattern of questions and answers would follow. "What do you do? Do you really like sushi? What do you do for fun?" My standard answer to the last question was, "I like to go up on the roof and fly my pigeons." This, I believed was a real turn-on for women.

Suddenly, all the intellectualization, both written and oral, with my selected potential significant others had ended. Somehow, I had winnowed a list of over fifty women who had displayed various modicums of interest in meeting me down to five possibilities. Like any good commander, I had three in reserve. With the help of a large desk calendar, various times and dates were filled in.

Over the course of the next two weeks, I was scheduled to meet five women for dinner. Logistics for this series of engagements were to be kept simple. In the small town I had relocated to, there was an Italian trattoria that felt like Tuscany inside. The food was consistently superb, and I could bring my own wine, thus saving a great deal of money.

My wife and I had frequented this restaurant since its inception over twenty years ago. Because it was her favorite, we dined there either alone or with numerous friends at least weekly. Once we had children, we simply took them along and put them under the table. The staff adored children. Now my kids take my grandchildren there regularly.

My last visit had been about one year after my wife died. Friends who thought this would help bring me out of my torpor had invited me there. No luck. Mario, the owner chef, another Mario, the waiter, and José, the assistant chef, all came over to express their condolences and tried to welcome me back into the fold. I felt so sad being there without my beloved wife that I had not thought about returning until now.

By sheer coincidence, or perhaps maybe not, the apartment I chose was less than two city blocks from the trattoria. I decided that this would be the jump-off spot in the quest for the impossible dream. I am sure my wife had a hand in this and was patiently waiting for the play to begin.

Suddenly, I was seventeen again! My God, five dates in less than two weeks! This was more action than I had in two years during my prime hunting days. I started to prepare for the upcoming safari. I slicked my hair with Brylcreem, thought about carrying an oh-so-cool pack of Luckies with my Zippo lighter, and—best of all—checked myself in the mirror and noted that there were no blackheads, zits, or incipient pimples. I was now a seventeen-year-old with at least sixty years' experience in the art of dealing with women (naive thought number one).

I suddenly realized that the simple perils of jungle-trekking—such as crossing leech-infested streams a la Humphrey Bogart in *The African Queen*; the possibility of becoming infested by a fifteen-foot-long tapeworm, which I had once seen in a pathology lab during medical school; or stumbling into an Ebola-infected village—were all minor compared to the greatest peril of all...*rejection.*

How would I, a man of sixty-plus years, who was so suave and sophisticated—a virtual Fred Astaire and Noel Coward combined—deal with this terrible prospect? I pushed this thought to the back of my mind when I remembered "the preparation of the wallet." In my teenage and early college years, all of the males usually had a thick wallet, full not with credit cards, as they were non-existent, but with telephone numbers, dollar bills, and other useless junk. In addition, each wallet, when folded and viewed from the outside, displayed a faint circular protuberance of about one inch in diameter. This distortion was caused by a solitary, aged, moldy, and obviously never-used condom. This vital piece of equipment could be found at all times in all the wallets I ever saw.

Obtaining a condom in those days of innocence was an ordeal. After slinking into a pharmacy in a distant part of town where the pharmacist did not know your mother, you waited until all the customers had gone, made sure no women were around, and began to stammer to the kindly old pharmacist. You usually did not have to finish the sentence before the old gentleman would reach under the counter and produce a macho box of Sheiks. You then hurriedly stuffed the box into your jeans and ran out of the store, believing you would soon be back for a new supply, although in reality, the box would last for years.

Should I prepare the wallet? "No," I decided. In this day of designer condoms in various colors, shapes and—Oh, my God—even *flavors*, this was probably such an important decision that it was best left to the woman. Another terrible thought crossed my mind. In addition to the condoms, would I now have to stuff my wallet with those little blue pills? If so, how would I know *when the time was right* to take them, as the ad said? This was almost as bad as the bone-shaking chill I got fifty years ago. What if my mother found my wallet? Enough of such foolishness. It was time for chef Mario, waiter Mario, and number one.

CHAPTER TEN:

Should I Pack Pajamas?

A mong the items women list in their biographies is their
desire for a "travel companion."

I was a bit perplexed by this wish. I was under the
impression that a travel companion was a stern, middle-aged
woman with sensible shoes who was employed to escort
spoiled, extremely wealthy teenage girls on an extended trip
to the capitals of Europe in order to round out their negligible
academic achievements.

I had also thought of a travel companion as a female with
nursing training who dressed in a white uniform and was employed to push elderly wealthy women seated in high-backed,
ancient wooden wheelchairs around the decks of a luxury
cruise ship.

Why on earth would the women I was interested in request
me to accompany them on a tour of the capitals of Europe or
push them around in wheelchairs?

Obviously, I had to consider the more updated meaning
of the phrase. A "travel companion" in the online dating
universe is one who travelled either on land or sea with a
member of the opposite sex. These members were in no way

related and may not even know each other. Further research into the subject precluded new questions. Assuming that these trips lasted days, or even weeks, what happened at night? Were two rooms secured in hotels? Were two cabins rented on a cruise ship? Upon checking with tour operators and cruise-ship offices, the answer was always "no." In fact, travel companions enabled the cost of a vacation or cruise to be almost cut in half if two people occupied the same room or cabin.

As Louie said in *Casablanca*, I was "shocked, shocked." Were all the extensive preparations I had made in an attempt to achieve the impossible dream of no value? Within the concept of being a travel companion, all of this clever preparation would appear to be unnecessary. The bottom line was that two, perhaps compatible, male and female members would, for an extended period of time, share not only the same bedroom, but most probably the same bed. Gone were the problems of my single twin bed, not really a twin bed. Could all of this really work?

"Yes, it could," I was told by the tour and cruise booking offices.

What if the two were not compatible? What if a spat occurred? What if one was teamed up with a homicidal online-dating-service maniac who had an ice pick under her side of the bed? What if one member wanted out of this relationship while at sea?

The desire for travel companions, which if answered by the male members, appeared to present potential dangers for the female member who sought this type of relationship.

Some male members of our demographic would at times have to make a major investment in Viagra and ask to see results of medical exams checking for STDs. The opportunities for ice-pick damage as well as being tossed overboard were great, but the opportunity for easy dream fulfillment seemed possible. Like most other decisions in life, in order to receive maximum gains, one had to accept maximum risk.

CHAPTER 11:

Angela

All intelligence had been analyzed, the reconnaissance plans were complete, and I entered the objective trattoria at 1900 hours. No pygmies with poisoned blowgun darts were seen, and neither was my date, Angela. Chef Mario did a double take. We made eye contact immediately, and he signaled that no other hostiles were about.

"Doc," he blurted out, "it's been such a long time. Then it *was* you I saw walking by the restaurant the last few days."

He hugged me effusively, and visions of Charles de Gaulle entering Paris flashed before me.

"Sure enough, Mario. I finally sold my house and moved here just so I could eat your food every day." This was not pure hyperbole. My cooking skills consisted of opening innumerable cans of tuna and sardines followed by beer, Doritos, and Cote d'Or chocolate bars.

"Come, Doc. I put you at your regular table," Mario said as he grabbed my arm.

"Hold off, Mario. I am meeting someone else, and I want to make sure she is able to find me."

At 19:10 hours, the object of the mission arrived. To my amazement, Angela looked exactly like her photo. No computer photo enhancement here. She was a woman of about sixty, my height and weight, in a flattering black pantsuit. Of interest was the fact that I had made Angela's acquaintance through a predominantly Jewish dating site. She was Catholic and of Italian heritage. Strange…my wife was also Catholic. Coincidence? Who knows?

Mario suddenly returned, rolled his eyes, and looked first at me and then at Angela. Did he know something about Italian women that I did not know? At this point, my Fred Astaire/ Noel Coward coolness emerged. I stood up, introduced Angela to Mario as "my new good friend."

Within a few seconds, perhaps through some sort of mental grapevine, Mario the waiter and Jose the assistant chef came running. The eyeball rolling continued and introductions were made all around, while the seated patrons wondered who the new VIPs were.

We exchanged pleasantries until the food quickly arrived.

"Ang," I asked with a mouthful of linguine amatriciana, "how come a nice, Italian Catholic woman like you joined an online dating site that is mainly Jewish?"

"When my husband died several years ago, I did not know any single men," she said. "I have a lot of Jewish girlfriends, and they all advised me that if I wanted to get serious again, I should look for a Jewish guy."

"What makes Jewish guys such great catches?" I asked as a strand of broccoli rabe stuck to my chin.

"Because everyone knows Jews make great husbands. They don't drink as much as the Christian men, they don't beat their wives, they don't go hunting and play with guns. Their favorite activity is sitting and eating. They are really easy to keep happy. All you have to do is feed them lots of pasta with red sauce."

My linguini was in a deep red sauce.

"And what's more," she added, looking me straight in the eye, "they make great lovers."

I nearly choked on my garlic bread as visions of Jewish-Italian orgies passed in front of me.

"True, all true," I croaked. Was this a hint of what was yet to come?

The meal, the wine, the conversation, and Ang were all delightful. The only thing I remember that was different from dates that I had over forty years ago was that we both discussed our anti-hypertension medication and the need to follow low-salt diets.

Two pleasant hours flew by. No leeches, tapeworms, or symptoms of Ebola virus had appeared. The Pinot Grigio was gone, the plate of shared tiramisu was empty, and it was time to leave.

As I walked Ang to her car, I had one problem to solve. Was a kiss expected? Was it on the cheek or smack on the lips? Was the mouth kept open or closed? What about tongues? My God, it had been over forty years since I even remotely thought about this. Some behaviors do not lend themselves to description, so I move on.

Angela asked where I was parked, and I said that I had walked over. I told her I had been advised by the dating service never to enter a date's car after the initial meeting. It sounded as if I would run the risk of being abducted by the online homicidal maniac and my body would never be found.

Ang gave me a worried look. Finally she smiled and said, "You're a bit weird, but nice....Let's get together again."

CHAPTER 12:

Selma

I t is important for the senior who is new to online dating to realize that not all of the scheduled dates will be positive experiences. Some of the encounters will prove to be tedious and at times quite boring, but each should be viewed as a learning experience. In the fullness of time, one will encounter a date that may exceed all expectations.

This new online dating experience resembles the blind dates we all had many years ago. One never knew how it would turn out. Unfortunately, most of the ladies with whom I was fixed up did not meet my own expectations, and I am certain that many of the women I dated felt the same way about me. I do not recall having any repeat encounters with any of them.

The online dating service encounters, however, go several steps beyond the blind date model. First of all, we are presented with a photo that may or may not be current or accurate in showing what the date looks like at the present time. Pay particular attention to how prospective dates describe their weight in the biography. The phrase "a few extra pounds" can cover some weighty territory.

We also have the opportunity to send and receive e-mail messages before we meet our dates. In most cases, telephone communication has been made, and we are able to evaluate the clues that we received verbally, comparing them to the written biography. Also, we now have the overwhelming advantage of Internet search engines to vet our potential dates.

The following narrative describes a recent date that, unfortunately, was not all that I, in my *tongue hanging out of my mouth* social situation would have wanted.

Forty-eight hours had now passed since my date with Ang, and I was once again at the scene of battle in the trattoria. As it did the first time, the scene played itself out with the sudden appearance of the lead warrior, a local realtor named Selma.

There was the obligatory rolling of the staffs' eyes and immediate seating at my now-reserved table. I quickly looked about to see if any of the patrons had recognized me, as I was now obviously a very important person.

I began to feel like the local Don, and I also noticed that I had begun to affect a slight swagger. Would a pinky ring be required?

"Have you been here before?" Selma asked. "Everyone seems to be staring at us."

Perhaps it was the "few extra pounds" and the form-fitting pink pantsuit that Selma was wearing. I quickly dismissed this unkind thought. They were staring because they knew that I was a man of respect.

It's strange how, after a certain age, logic becomes more flexible and adapts itself to perceived needs. Even the rigid laws of thermodynamics do not hold true when a senior male goes out on dates.

I was working my way down the pasta dishes. Linguine amatriciana was now replaced with spaghetti puttanesca, probably a subliminal yearning for *the impossible dream.*

Selma was a pleasant woman who claimed to be sixty-five in her biography.

Age was only a *number,* though, and not to be taken seriously.

Things began pleasantly enough, but after thirty minutes or so, conversation seemed to drag; the spontaneity was not there. This was not all bad, as it allowed me to wolf down some great Tuscan bread and—oh my God—*butter.*

I concentrated on the pasta dish, paying particular attention to avoid biting into a black olive that still had a pit. This would not be a cool time to break a tooth. A Don would never let this happen.

Conversation had now started to limit itself to the areas of grandchildren and the difficulty of learning how to play golf. I tried to listen with interest, but the glazed-eye syndrome had begun. If pictures of grandchildren were forthcoming, maybe I could develop the well-known online dating migraine headache, or perhaps I could get my cell phone to ring by willing it to happen. Mercifully, the photographs were not produced. Golf has never been one of my favorite past times—neither talking about it, nor watching it on television, nor thinking that Tiger Woods was such a wonderful man and terrific role model.

Selma relished it. I learned about the correct swing and stance. Surprisingly, not too many better-accomplished golfers looked forward to a game with a grandmotherly neophyte. If it were not for the pinot and the great anchovies and capers in the pasta to spice things up, the evening was heading for total disaster.

Most remarkable, the impossible dream had withered. After thirty minutes more of this struggling on both sides, we agreed that it was late, people had to show open houses in the morning, and it was time for both of us to cut our losses and run (from each other).

I guess that this date epitomizes the lack-of-chemistry model. It was neither Selma's fault nor my own. We simply did not have anything in common to talk about. We existed on separate planets. Any physical attraction between us, if it indeed ever existed, was not relevant. There was no need to complain; we each had a fine meal, and the wine tended to smooth things out.

CHAPTER 13:

Too Much of a Good Thing

I took three days for some R&R, and then I reported to Mario's place for my next date. I was ten minutes early, with the obligatory bottle of wine. Again, the staff greeted me, but did I notice a certain sneer, a look of *insolence* at their Don? Pinky ring or not, unless all due respect was shown, some messages in the form of newspaper-wrapped mackerel could easily be delivered. If behavior did not change, one could find oneself *sleeping with the fishes.* "Enough foolish thoughts," I told myself.

Tonight was to be a most enjoyable evening that had marked potential for *dream achievement.* After all, was I not meeting Joyce, a practicing psychiatrist who had even attended the same medical school as I? She would, no doubt, be a very savvy Brooklyn-born woman who, thanks to her training, would know all about fantasies and their required fulfillment. We would first renew old times at the school, talk about the various professors, and have some wine. Then I, in my sophisticated way, would mention the nearby apartment and old collection of medical school yearbooks. This would all be totally irresistible to an old medical school colleague, I thought—foolish, naive idea number two.

I had worked my way down the pasta list, and tonight, aptly enough, it was linguine ala zingara. The conversation flowed easily, but, to my horror, started to soar to insane intellectual heights. We discussed not apartments and fantasy fulfillment, but the use of metaphors in clinical psychiatric practice. We then played a sick game, trying to outdo each other by speaking only in tricky metaphors. Seeking to impress Joyce with my unbelievable intelligence after a couple of glasses of wine, I mentioned that I was one of the few people I ever knew who had read and even understood Joyce's *Ulysses*. I thought the play of her first name and the author's last name was indeed so clever.

Both of us were decompensating rapidly, secondary to the mega-dose of mutual intelligence. I had somehow transcended the concept of *the dream*, and was now in a far higher parallel reality not contaminated by matters sexual. From Joyce, I went on to chaos theory, entropy, and the laws of thermodynamics. "These were all I believed in," I told Joyce. She agreed with everything I said. I then knew that I was in the presence of a remarkably intelligent physician.

The restaurant had started to empty, the staff was shooting me more disrespectful looks, and it was time to go. *The dream* would have to keep, and the mackerel had to be wrapped.

I found it hard to believe that I had done three women in one week. Please note that the word *done* is not meant in the vernacular sense in which I employed it as a seventeen-year-old. It now meant the completion of the initial date with a real live female. *Two more to go...*or so I thought.

Of the initial five candidates, two remained. I was almost too emotionally spent to complete my mission. Luck, however, was with me. Approximately three hours before the standard assigned time of a seven o'clock liaison, I received a pathetic call from my potential date. It appeared that she was gardening in her five-acre flower patch when she bent down to pull a weed. Instead, she pulled her back and thought that immediate and prolonged bed rest was essential. She was very sorry not to be able to meet me, but she was sure I would understand how important it was to lie down instead. Would I call her back in a week or two? Perhaps by then she would be recovered. I assured her of my deep concern for her acute malady and promised a rain date in the coming millennium.

Prospective Woman Number Five called about one day prior to our scheduled rendezvous. "Miracle of miracles," she said. Evidently, reconciliation had occurred with her boyfriend, and she would no longer be available for trysts with me or anyone else. I still continued, however, to receive her tantalizing photo and biographical material as a potential match via email. Obviously, she was keeping her options open.

Ah, well. As a quite sophisticated online dating service member, I accepted both stories with the aplomb they required. Some have the good sense to back out of a safari before the goat-eating anaconda gets them.

It is important, though, to learn how to accept and cope with rejection. Forty years ago, I was quite adept at this and was usually able to hold back the tears until I shut myself in the bathroom. It only took about two hours for me to emerge, bearing swollen red eyes and a determination to remain celibate. (At this stage in my life, celibacy was no problem.) I now find rejection to be not such a problem either. I suffer from dry-eye syndrome, and frequent sobbing is beneficial.

During the following week, I re-contacted both Ang and Joyce, and we made plans to meet again. The venue was changed, as I began to suspect that another New Jersey *family* was muscling in on my *cosa*. Conveniently, a fair Thai restaurant was just a short stroll away from my apartment. Pad Thai and red and green curry replaced pasta. Wine gave way to six-packs of imported Asian beer. The relationships remained easy and pleasant and, as the online group said, "You have to wait and see how things develop." I was not sure if this included *the dream*, but I remained a confirmed optimist.

I took time during this lull in my hectic social calendar to visit my internist, Mark, who was my roommate during internship, for my physical. Unbelievably, a few days later, I received a telephone call from him.

"Bush," he bellowed. (Mark was all of six-and-a-half feet tall and quite formidable when angry.) "What the hell is going on? Your ankles were swollen when I saw you, and the results just came in. Aside from your blood pressure being off the wall, your lipids are lousy, and your blood sugar is almost two hundred."

Could eight or nine pounds of pasta, at least half a case of wine, several six-packs of beer, and unrestricted salt intake all within two weeks do this?

"Mark," I said, "I have started to socialize again, and I guess I have been overdoing it."

"Overdoing it?" he yelled. "I suppose your primary goal is to get laid as much as possible. Let me tell you, my friend, you will no doubt experience ED. And when you come to me for the pills, I am going to say, as they do on television, that 'you are not fit to engage in sexual activity.'"

"Mark," I promised, "anything but that. I have seen the light and will behave. Just cheap coffee dates from now on."

I am sure that this was all said to shock me back to being in my sixties instead of thinking I was now seventeen. Nevertheless, my quest for *the impossible dream* would continue, assuming I could lace up my shoes over my swollen feet.

CHAPTER 14:

Initial Date Rules of Engagement

Once you have settled on the time and place for your first date, several problems may arise when you first meet the female member. I have experienced some of these and a little advice is in order.

On the initial date, I make a point of arriving at least five or ten minutes prior to the scheduled meeting time. This is a gallant maneuver. The woman should not have to stand alone in a bar or restaurant, nervously searching about for me. However, a problem immediately comes to mind: How will I recognize my date?

When initially making dates, I thought about using my innate David Niven panache and informing the lucky women that I would have a white carnation pinned to my lapel. But white carnations—and even lapels—are a thing of the past. Men, especially those of a certain age, do not wear flowers on dates. Just being there, waiting to meet an unknown woman, was foolishness enough.

Another ploy of equal sophistication could have been to sit at a small table near the entrance with a solitary Martini glass before me. My date would certainly have no trouble spotting the urbane gentleman elegantly seated behind a long-stemmed crystal Martini glass. This ploy appealed to me; however, should my partner arrive late, I would be well into my second or even third drink and would not make a terrific first impression. Anyway, I studied the up-to-date photos of the women I was soon to meet and believed that there would be no problem in identifying them. How naive I was!

At this early stage in dating, I still had not appreciated the fact that online daters, both male and female, are experts in the art of extending the truth and cleverly fashioning little white lies.

From personal experience, I know now that most photos are at best a rough approximation of how the member really looks. One should add at least five years and, just to be sure, sometimes ten years.

Most women, at least the ones I dated, are really not "slim and slender," as described in their biographies. Neither are they "athletically fit." In most cases, their weight is left blank in the submitted database. If you add about fifteen or twenty pounds to the photo, together with an age correction, you at least have a fighting chance of identifying your date.

Once identities have been ascertained, hands shaken, and perhaps a kiss or two on the cheek exchanged, male members should compliment the women and tell them how much prettier they are than their photos. Do not forget to do this. It may bear compound interest in the future.

An additional unexpected problem I had after several dates was remembering names. Most of the women in my demographic have rather simple, uncomplicated names such as Alice, Barbara, Elaine, Susan, Sheila, etc. The dating site women have remarkable hearing and would pick up a name error while I was still on the first syllable. What I found terribly hard to overcome were the *Sh* names, such as Sheila or Sherry. I had an easier time early in the meeting if I chose a non-identifying name such as "dear, sweetie, blue eyes," or any other idiotic name I could get away with.

When the check appears, and the date offers to pay half, do not be a typical gallant moron and insist on paying the entire bill, as I was prone to do early in my dating career. It took me a long time to realize this was not necessary, and the learning experience was expensive. Times are different now. More than likely, you have retired and are living on a fixed income. The women, however, are probably younger than you, are still working, and earning staggering incomes.

Handling the check may prove to be problematic because of male vanity. In a dimly lit restaurant or bar, especially those illuminated with flattering candlelight, there is no way we men in our demographic are able to decipher the check without reading glasses. Naturally, we do not have these with us, since we are *oh so cool* and do not want our dates to think we are over forty-five.

If you are determined to maintain this ploy, I offer the following solution" When the bill comes, depending on the elegance of the restaurant, pay with cash. Simply pull out a hundred dollar bill or a fifty that you have previously placed in an accessible part of your wallet. This will invariably cover the bill, and when the change comes, you can mentally calculate what the evening has cost and how much tip to leave.

Assuming the date has gone well and you have jumped all of the hurdles, one possible problem remains—can you remember where you parked?

CHAPTER 15:

The Evolution of Online Dating

ark's phone call shocked me back into reality. Was online dating the magic elixir sought by Ponce de Leon? Did it really have the ability to transport sixty- and seventy-year-olds back to their youth? Did online dating sites, with their untold thousands of women, each seeking a man, affect the hormonal stability of senior men? All one had to do was log on, say "Open, Sesame," and click a heart, to immediately notify female member of an online dating service that a man was interested.

Multitudes of women awaited me, as did untold plates of pasta, sauces galore, casks of wine, and kegs of beer. The bounty appeared endless. I, who at the age of seventeen had to struggle mightily for a date, was now inundated by scores of women who fought for the chance to meet me. The demographics had suddenly changed. All the good-looking, athletic men of my youth, the ones who kicked sand in my face at the beach, were now underground.

Darwin was right! It is "survival of the fittest," and I was now among the fittest. My self-confidence soared, but in the back of mind I harbored the vague concern that perhaps these online dating services were like the 1940s radio program, *The Shadow*. Was it Lamont Cranston who had the ability to "cloud men's minds"? Had I suddenly entered a parallel universe? Was anything here real? Surely my phone call to the guru would answer these questions. Armed with a non-alcoholic beer and a bag of no-salt-added potato chips, I placed my call.

The Sibyl listened patiently while I told my tale. Rather proudly, I detailed my accomplishments in the short span of only a few weeks. Suddenly, out of the blue, she asked a question and used a phrase I had not heard in over forty years.

"Are you getting much?" Who would even pose such a question to a suave, sophisticated pillar of the community who was a retired, kindly old physician? After I fumbled for an answer, she quietly said, "Enough. Let me continue."

Did I notice a change in the cadence of her voice? A more transcendent tone? The beginning of a revelation?

"You have been trained in scientific method," began the Sibyl. "You are, therefore, aware that the rate of scientific progress is exponential. Online dating sites are merely a new technology being used to make the meeting of males and females easier, less time intensive, and less dependent on largely insane and archaic methods of courtship. These sites represent the first primitive steps to a process that, in the not-too-distant future, will be based on a planet-wide database.

"In time to come, all residents on earth will be part of a complete database. This will include the person's complete genome and a totality of their physical and emotional data points. These will include obvious physical measurements to the evaluation of mental and emotional health secured during deep psychological interviews. When the time for mating or emotional bonding occurs, a simple mouse click by the parties of interest will result in a match such as is not even a vague idea at this time."

"Enough of the future, Sibyl," I begged, "I need help in the present."

At once her voice changed. She was no longer HAL, the disembodied computer in *2001: A Space Odyssey*. "OK, Marty, let's turn to specifics. There are many online dating sites. Some cater to different religions, others to certain age groups, and most to all comers. They are all a mixture of people seeking significant others, people with normal, healthy thought processes, many disturbed people, predators (as I have previously described), and a large number of individuals, both male and female, who enjoy playing the dating game but will never complete the process.

"For them, the chase is important, not the capture. Only a miniscule percentage of the total membership of any site will ever achieve their goals. Many will be happy with a single date; others will require the total commitment of marriage. The one factor that all members have in common is loneliness. They are searching for a remedy for this condition and are willing to subject themselves and, at times, pay a significant fee, to overcome this malady, which can be terrible.

"You are part of this group. You seek a level of both emotional and physical fulfillment that the online site may or may not provide you. The individual you seek is most probably in the site database. The site will help with the demographics and narrow the field.

"Whether or not you will succeed in your quest," the oracular voice suddenly returned, "is up to you, in small part, and to the Fates, in larger measure. Continue your quest; cut down on pasta, wine, and beer. Think less carnally, although in your case this may be difficult. The demographics are in your favor. And "may the force be with you!"

CHAPTER 16:

Lhasa

E very so often, while skimming through female members'
biographies and photos, one will stand out from the rest.
Such was the case with a member whose screen name
was "Lhasa."

"A rather unusual name for a woman of Ashkenazi decent,"
I thought.

This would require further investigation. In her intriguing
biography, Lhasa stated that she was a sixty-year-old woman
who had never married; at this point in time, she was seeking
a long-term relationship or marriage. Her photo revealed a
handsome woman in multiple poses, dressed in very colorful
silk dresses. One photo pictured her lying full length on a silk
divan, semi-clad in a silk kimono. The pose was reminiscent
of the voluptuous female nude painted by Goya in his work
sometimes referred to as "The Naked Maja." I was now totally
ensnared.

Her listed accomplishments included fluency in multiple
Asian languages, such as Mandarin Chinese, Tibetan, Korean,
Vietnamese, and Japanese.

"Wow," said I, and read on. She had done years of fieldwork in Tibet, and one of her most remarkable achievements was finding and unearthing an ancient Buddhist temple. Lhasa spent about six months per year doing fieldwork in Tibet and other Asian countries, and the remainder of the year she taught in the Asian Studies department at a major Ivy League university. Lhasa had published multiple papers in her field as well as several books, and she lectured frequently about her work at numerous academic institutions. Lhasa, I also learned, was the capital of Tibet.

This was one woman I had to meet. I imagined that many male members of dating services would find such an accomplished woman quite intimidating. Not me, though. After all, I spoke at least ten words of Vietnamese.

I clicked the "yes" button, the pink heart lit up, and I was off. I then forwarded a complimentary e-mail to her, expressing my interest and admiration for all she had accomplished. Upon reevaluating her photo, I thought that I detected a slight epicanthic fold in her eyelids characteristic in those of Asian descent.

Lhasa sent a return e-mail thanking me for my compliments and said she felt that I, too, was quite an interesting member of that particular dating service. With this groundwork completed, I proceeded to the next level. I e-mailed my full name and telephone number to her and asked her to call me if she felt comfortable with this jump to the next level.

The next day, the phone rang. A woman named Susan asked, "Are you Marty?"

"Yes," I said, detecting a slight accent in her voice. "You sound quite charming, but do I know you?"

"You probably know me better as Lhasa," the caller said.

Wow, I thought. This was going to be one heck of an interesting conversation. The mysteries of the Orient would be revealed to me; I had always wanted to date an Asian woman. My sister's eyes would really bug out when she saw me with this exotic, silk-clad beauty.

"Lhasa, or maybe I should call you Susan," I said. "What a great pleasure it is to speak with you." A rather long conversation ensued. I learned of her fascinating fieldwork in Tibet at an elevation of over ten thousand feet in the Himalayas. She described living in yurts, riding yaks, eating yaks, drinking yak milk, and unearthing lost Buddhist treasures.

It was time now to fill in the blanks. "Lhasa," I said, preferring that name to Susan, "I detect a slight accent. Am I right?"

She paused. "A slight accent?" she said. "I was born and raised in New Jersey."

"But you look so exotic in all those lovely silks, and all the languages you speak, and your lovely eyelids and all. Surely you must be putting me on."

"Marty," she said, "I am a New Jersey girl. In fact I was born, raised, and went to high school in a town about ten miles from where you live now."

"But how did you learn to speak all those languages?" I asked. "And how did you get those epicanthic folds?"

"What's an epicanthic fold?" she asked.

I tried to explain the anatomical nuances of the fold, but she laughed.

"And you practiced ophthalmology?" She giggled. "I learned to speak the various languages on the job. When I was in Tibet, I was totally immersed; in order to eat, I learned."

I was starting to hear the air hissing out of my overblown Asian fantasy. "But all those exquisite silk clothes?" I croaked.

"When I was in the Orient, over the course of years, I brought back lots of bolts of raw silk and had them tailored locally," she said.

The escaping air kept hissing much louder now. "So you're really not Tibetan? You don't have epicanthic folds? But you look so exotic and desirable lying on the silk divan wrapped in all that silk," I whispered hoarsely.

Another giggle. "Marty, what a great imagination you have. I might also add that I am one heck of a great cook when it comes to authentic Asian dishes. I did notice in your biography that you liked Asian cuisine."

"Yes, yes. I love it, I love it, I love everything Asian, especially sweet and sour yak, and most of all, lovely New Jersey-Asian women who lie with their arms akimbo, semi-clothed on silk divans," I croaked faintly. I had been practically deflated, but now things began to improve as my fantasy returned anew.

"Lhasa," I panted, "we have to meet. The only problem is that I had to stop driving awhile ago, and I see you live about thirty or so miles away."

There was a long silence. Then she said, "Marty, I never felt the need to drive. I always lived in large cities and was out of the country for long periods of time."

"My God!" I mentally screamed. There are no cabs where I live. Would I be the first male ever to hire a car and driver to meet an online date?

We ended our lengthy call, promising to try to come up with a solution to the mobility problem.

"Perhaps a yak," she suggested. "I have no trouble driving them."

***

Unfortunately, it was difficult for me to realize that in online dating, it is common to split the costs of the date. Foolishly, I insisted on paying all the costs. I used the old Jimmy Stewart phrase, "Shucks, ma'am, I'm just an old-fashioned kind of fella."

The women I dated did not seem to mind too much, but after a while my gallantry started to become expensive. After all, I was living on the monthly allowance my financial planner, Lucretia, had decided was adequate when I first consulted her. Things had radically changed, however. I was now a social butterfly who frequented nightspots, restaurants, and bars with gay abandon and different women at least twice per week. My credit card balance had started to balloon, and I realized painfully that some action had to be taken.

A call or perhaps even a visit to Lucretia was indicated. I was intimidated by the prospect, but after all, she worked for me and I was in charge (or so I thought foolishly). An appointment was made and off I went.

Lucretia sported a new eyeshade and looked at me with her gimlet eye.

"What brings you back so soon, Martin?" was her greeting.

"I think that we have to adjust my monthly distribution, as I keep running out of money. I have started to socialize, and taking out women is expensive."

An expression that could have passed for a smile flickered across her enigmatic face. "I thought you were beyond that foolishness," she cackled.

"Not so; definitely not so," I croaked. I explained that men in my age group were in great demand by women because there were so few of us around. "Most of those in my age group," I said with a satisfied smile, "are dead, senile, in diapers, or totally impotent." I also mentioned that since the advent of Viagra, more and more men were now sexually active. A blush overcame me, and I started to shrink in my chair.

Lucretia smirked and began to toy with her very sharp number-two pencil. "You do remember, don't you, that you agreed to a contract, a contract even sealed in blood? Are you aware of the high incidence of leg fractures in those who break contracts?"

"Yes. Yes," I croaked, thinking of how difficult it would be to go on dates with crutches. I now realized that coming to this spider's web was not a brilliant idea.

Lucretia continued, "Aside from possible orthopedic expenses, which probably are not covered by Medicare, there are other things to consider. If I am forced to invade principle, and you are foolish enough to live longer than you should, certain things will happen. You will soon find yourself in state-subsidized senior housing complete with roaches, rats, and an incoherent, probably incontinent roommate watching endless reruns of *I Love Lucy*. You will learn to like several brands of cat food, and you will become proficient at making paper flowers in the dayroom. Is this what you really want, Martin?"

I started to grovel on the floor. "No, no; anything but the "golden years." Please forgive me, Godmother, for my foolish thoughts."

Lucretia eyed me coldly. "Martin," she said, "you will be forgiven only this once, but there may come a day when your Godmother will come to you and ask you to perform a small service for her."

"Anything, anything," I groveled, picking my head up to kiss her ring.

The day of the big spender had ended, but at least the crutches would not be necessary.

CHAPTER 17:

East Side Max

After dating several members of an online dating site, I noticed a new pattern emerging in my behavior and expectations during these meetings.

As a teenager, and even in my twenties, physical appearance and feminine beauty were of prime importance. My friends and I did not want to go out with or even be seen spending too much time with a young lady who did not meet certain standards of good looks.

In retrospect I now realize how sexist, immature, and ridiculous this behavior was. We, the males, were not uniformly handsome. Many of us were overweight or gangly; we had acne and rotten, narcissistic personalities. All of this completely changed with the onset of my dating experience as a senior.

While still paying some attention to the physical appearance of my date, especially when meeting and identifying her for the first encounter, appearance was not important to me.

What I found far more important was the warmth, understanding, and ease of conversation with the woman. A bit of extra weight, wrinkles, and other dermatologic stigmata sometimes present in a woman of a certain age had absolutely no relevance. What was important now was the inner beauty.

During the most successful meetings, it did not take long for both of us to decide if this encounter would truly blossom into something deeper. It was apparent to me that the women seemed to feel the same way about the presence or lack of physical attributes in their dates. They were far more interested in kindness, consideration, and being treated as the accomplished women they were.

I do not mean to denigrate physical beauty; however, like all things subject to evaluation, the metrics used by seniors tend to change over time.

There are, of course, exceptions to any perceived changes in behavior. During one dinner date with a pretty, articulate woman, I asked a question that I had asked all the women I had met: What were her most memorable experiences with online dating?

Florence related the following story:

"A bio was forwarded to me describing a male member in his sixties who used the screen name 'East Side Max.' In his bio, he said that he lived in New York, was a retired engineer, and was interested in a long-term relationship. His picture showed a tall man with a pleasant face and a charming smile. Although I live in New Jersey and normally do not consider it worthwhile to travel thirty miles to New York City for an initial date, the chance to meet East Side Max appealed to me.

"I bucked traffic to the east side of Manhattan and parked in a terribly expensive garage, since there was no street parking. East Side Max was waiting for me in a coffee shop. We introduced ourselves and sat down at a small table.

"Max lived up to his bio and photo. He was quite good-looking and courteous, at least at the beginning. We sat opposite each other and started to talk. As the minutes wore on, I noticed that Max, who was originally seated directly opposite me, was moving closer and closer. The room was noisy, and I just thought that moving closer helped him hear me better.

"To my horror, I suddenly felt his hand grab my thigh under the table! I immediately jumped up out of my seat and shouted, 'What are you doing?' People at other tables looked at us. I felt embarrassed, and Max gradually slid away.

"I was uncertain what to do next, so I continued the conversation as though this had been a slight aberration and now Max had learned his limits. After another five minutes of conversation, Max suddenly stood up.

"'Florence,' he said. 'Both of us are mature adults. We both know or should know that sexual intimacy is an integral part of any relationship between adults. Frankly, I am shocked, *shocked* at your childlike unsophisticated behavior. I was just trying to show you affection, and you rejected me.'

"'But this is a first date!' I told him.

"'Florence, you need to think this over. You have my number. When you come to your senses, give me a call.'

"The next thing I knew," Florence said, "he stood up and walked out of the restaurant, leaving me with the bill. What do you think of that?" Florence asked me.

This was dangerous territory for me. Although I did not condone Max's behavior, it had a certain no-nonsense panache. I would assume that his grope had achieved positive results before, and short-term relationships were his specialty.

I tried to answer truthfully, although I could see that Florence was upset. I knew that a flippant, humorous reply would be a mistake.

"Florence," I said, "I would take his unseemly behavior as a compliment. Here you are, a woman of *a certain age* who apparently—and it is *most* obvious to me—is extremely attractive to men!" I noticed a slight smile come over her face. It was all I could do to control myself and not reach under the table and grab her thigh.

CHAPTER 18:

A New Metric of Beauty

The time has come, the Walrus said,
To talk of many things,
Of shoes and ships and sealing wax,
Of cabbages and kings.
Lewis Carroll, Alice in Wonderland

The time has also come for this walrus to describe the correct and proper way to conduct an online-sponsored date. In previous chapters, I have attempted to maintain a jocular narrative of my own experiences with online dating.

It is now time to convey, at least for a short while, a more serious tone. I believe that most people join an online dating service as a last resort. Some members of these sites may consider themselves failures because they did not find a partner using normal methods of social interaction, such as at school, work, or through a professional matchmaker. To have to pay to join a site and be marketed with photograph and biography may feel demeaning and produce anxiety. The vast majority of members in our age group, myself included, have suffered a grievous and at times catastrophic loss of a mate through death or a wrenching, emotionally charged divorce.

We are all fragile people. We are all seeking to establish a new reality, hopefully with a new partner. We are emotionally labile, especially in our decision-making. Our ability to evaluate new potential partners is often subject to error. Hopefully, we will become aware of potentially devastating decisions before the relationship deepens. There may be unresolved guilt associated with dating, particularly in those who have suffered spousal loss.

Our friends and family may consider joining these sites unwise. Perhaps some perceive these actions as showing a loss of faith to a departed wife or husband. The decision, however, is ours alone. Once we make it, a new and perhaps dangerous world of conflicting emotions awaits us. It is incumbent upon all members to treat those members in whom they show interest with dignity and respect.

Primum non nocere. First do no harm. We, as members, have now revealed our deepest feelings, yearnings, and innermost emotional thoughts to thousands who care to read them. We have responded to personal questions that, in reality, should be known only in the context of a loving relationship. My God, we are even encouraged to reveal our weight, income, and zodiac sign!

While we may fabricate harmlessly with answers about age, hair color, or body type, photographs included, the essays we write concerning emotional content are not fabrications or hyperbole. They are what we think, what we desire, what we yearn to achieve, and who we are. They have been freely and honestly written and must be carefully dealt with by the other members.

At the age of seventeen, exuberant breast size was our chief interest and desire. The most common question my friends and I asked each other when arranging dates was, "Does she have big tits?" Other pertinent factors such as number of limbs, heartbeat, and respiration were of secondary importance. Nothing could compare with breast size.

Fast-forward forty years, and the breast conundrum persists. But now there are both positive as well as negative parameters. The good news is that in the age group in which we men now swim, the women we date are overwhelmingly endowed with large, full breasts, probably in some cases twice the mass of our teenage dates. The cleavages in which once we could lose our hands have deepened to the point where now we could lose our entire arm.

There is, however, my dear male reader, a new dimension. In the group we seek, not only is breast size uniformly large, but also there is length. This is something we never dreamed of forty years ago. A breast reaching almost to the waist or even further was a visual none of us ever considered. The possibilities of what I would call "breast play" are now staggering. Who says, "An old dog learns no new tricks"?

One must realize, however, that the folks we are interested in, and intend to meet, will be slightly different from the young, nubile, clear-skinned, firm-breasted girls who for the most part had all their teeth. One must now accept facts that may not be immediately evident, but will become so if and when a relationship is established and has begun to deepen.

First among these facts is the changing concept of feminine beauty. The women we meet, although in our minds still young and vibrant, will come with a patina. Skin is a living organ; like heart, lung, or kidney, it undergoes physiologic change with the passage of time. This fact should appear obvious, but we, as men, try to discount it. The women presented to us at this juncture are as beautiful and vibrant as those we once dealt with, but in a different way.

Their skin may display wrinkles, occasional surgical scars, brown age spots, a devilish hair follicle, deep lines along lips and eyes, redundant discolored skin on the eyelids, a missing tooth or two, and excessive subcutaneous tissue on the neck and arms. The bosom, as I have detailed, will be adequate in all dimensions, but there will be instances in which one or both may be absent. This is not to be viewed as a cosmetic blemish; it is a fact of life and must be accepted as such. The sign of a true, caring, and mature man is how he treats this situation. One must proceed with the utmost care and show no evidence of discomfort or queasiness. Women with this condition have suffered enough physical and emotional pain.

Do not be afraid, should the occasion arise, to fondle this area; pay special attention in a manly manner to what may or may not be left. You know what I mean, guys; think back to what you did as a seventeen-year-old. There may be scars, both mental and physical, which were not present forty years ago. Keep in mind that you, as well, are neither a Greek Adonis nor Michael Jordan.

All of what I have described represents only ephemeral beauty. The true beauty of the woman is anatomically located beneath the skin. The inner beauty of the person never ages and is always there if we have enough brains and ambition to seek it.

An important ingredient in this new concept of online dating is to recognize and praise what remains. One can never be too complimentary. These women want to be loved; they want to be appreciated for who they are and for what they have achieved. Both of you have been given another chance at a possible transcendent relationship. Do not squander it on idiotic teenage fantasies.

CHAPTER 19:

First-Date Fantasies

Ever the optimist, believing hoards of women would soon be making their way to my place for a nightcap, I now gave thought to the preparation of my apartment.

It would be only a short period of time, I thought, before I would use that famous line I had heard thousands of times in the movies of my youth. You know that line—where the good-looking, suave male turns to the glamorous woman in the back of the Checker cab and says, "Would you care to come up for a nightcap, my dear?"

In my case, inevitable success of this ploy was preordained. Did I not, in the course of ten years, own two Checker cabs, one for myself in white and the other in yellow for my wife? People considered us strange, but the cars were the best we had ever owned. Roomy, with big engines, they attracted attention wherever we went.

A favorite perverse activity of ours was driving the yellow one through Manhattan and watching people trying to flag us down. Since I owned two such vehicles, Checker Motors considered me a "small-fleet owner." I received special discounts. Best of all, I was allowed to have the cars serviced at the official Checker Taxi Repair Facility in the wilderness of Queens. There I had the great opportunity of meeting and talking "taxi" with the other drivers who, at that time, spoke English. I learned the best routes for getting around the city and where to find public restrooms on almost every block. Several West Side diners allowed only us elite taxi drivers to sit at the counter. My wife and I lapped it up.

But I digress. The taxis are long gone, Checker Motors became a financial service company, and the old-time drivers gradually died off, to be replaced by non-English-speaking immigrants. The roomy cabs themselves were replaced with cramped, dirty, small, domestic compacts.

My apartment, though, still contained vestiges of the golden years of New York taxidom. I had two Checker hubcaps, which I mounted proudly on the wall, and a wonderful yellow teapot shaped like a Checker cab, festooned with checkerboard logo, which poured tea out of a spout in its radiator. Romantic objects of a bygone era, these items, I believed, would be of immense interest to any female who decided to respond to my suave invitation. This was naive thought number three.

A small problem, however, did exist with furniture. There was none. I had moved out of my basement with the minimum of possessions. All I carried with me were a sideboard, a chest of drawers, a television, and one half of a twin bed set. I had already ordered some new furniture, but because I had requested bright-red leather upholstery, it would take the Chinese about three months to fabricate it. Not to worry. I still had one old armchair and a camp chair that we used to take to the beach.

The bed, however, might present a problem. This did not weigh too heavily on my mind, since the apartment came with new wall-to-wall carpet. This afforded much more room than half of a twin bed, I thought. No doubt this would be immensely appealing to a woman in her sixties who would see the value of lying on the floor in order to relieve some of her arthritis.

I paid particular attention to the bathroom, putting out the freshest of the two towels I had, making sure the toilet paper roll was full, and even putting a spare roll over the toilet ledge. Was I cool or not? The rubber toilet plunger was strategically placed in the tub and the shower curtain drawn. A bathroom fit for the queen!

The kitchen appeared to be in reasonable shape, since it did not get much use. The stereo was wired and set to play pop and romantic music of the 1960s. The ten-disc set that I had ordered after watching a TV infomercial would set the perfect mood.

I had wine ready. Appetizers would consist of low-salt pretzels and potato chips. I even had a container of mixed olives. Instead of napkins, several sheets of paper towels were neatly stacked, and an ashtray was provided for the olive pits.

At the last minute, though, a dreadful thought occurred to me. I did not know where the wine opener was. To my relief, one of the bottles had a screw cap.

Excellent. All was ready, and the troops were deployed. All that remained was a rather simple battle tactic, I thought: to utter the magic line when my next date would approach the ambush site.

Most of the online dating sites offer very precise instructions for that all-important first date. Members are encouraged to meet on a bright, sunny day in a public place—like the lobby of a police station—with lots of other people about. The sites also urge members to make certain the area is not confined and has multiple exits. Presumably, these suggestions are made in an attempt to protect members from the occasional homicidal date. With luck, the member may be able to escape by becoming lost in the crowd or, hopefully, by making it to a nearby exit.

Online dating sites also instruct members not to have first dates in the evening, especially when the moon is full. Should dates be inevitable during a full moon, it would not be amiss to place a small clove of garlic strategically in the cleavage or a shirt pocket. Under no circumstances should the members arrange to meet by traveling together in a vehicle. Each member should make sure to arrive in his or her own car.

There have been several unfortunate reports of female members winding up in a brothel in Montenegro or in Yemeni harems. Several male members have found themselves awakening in various hospital intensive care units after the involuntary donation of a kidney. Pay attention to these suggestions. The sites know of what they speak.

As I have mentioned before, I have difficulty with how to split the bill at the end of the date. I consider it tacky to "go Dutch," but now find myself looking at the pet food shelves at the supermarket, as my disposable income shrinks.

The mathematical calculation of bill splitting is fraught with danger. Suppose one member has a second drink or—even worse—orders from the right side of the menu? Should the other member take note of this at the time the bill is presented and calculate how much each has eaten and had to drink so that an equitable reckoning can be made? Is it considered more correct to just split the bill down the middle? Who determines how much the tip should be? There is a potential for strife if one member is a fifteen-percent tipper and the other tips twenty percent. Thus, I find it easier to pay the bill in its entirety, although at times this has produced much pain in the wallet. My suggestion is for both members to throw their credit cards on the table and let the waiter figure it out.

At rare times, this bill payment may not present any problems. The "online migraine attack" has been known to appear without warning, and the afflicted member may suddenly stand up, shriek, and run out of the establishment. In these cases, at least you get to finish her drink and maybe even take some food home in a doggy bag.

This represents a small part of the learning curve in dealing with online dating. However, the true dater will, in the fullness of time, be able to arrange trysts in his or her apartment. It is convenient to order take-out Chinese food or a ten-dollar pizza. In this ideal situation, one saves money, saves time looking for a parking spot, and only Lamont Cranston ("the Shadow") knows "what evil lurks in the hearts of men."

CHAPTER 20:

I Won't Dance; Don't Ask Me

Female members of online dating sites often list ballroom dancing as one of their interests.

Dancing? Could this be true, or is it just an example of feminine hyperbole? I found it hard to picture women in their sixties and seventies, most probably afflicted with arthritic hips and knees and swollen ankles, their feet festooned with bunions and safely encased in sturdy black leather specially-made shoes laced along the side, seriously considering themselves able to glide effortlessly about the dance floor. Had Lamont Cranston visited them with his ability to "cloud minds" while they were drafting their biographies?

I suddenly had a mental picture of a bevy of aged women vigorously dancing with their walkers as portrayed in Mel Brooks's Broadway show, *The Producers*. Had Max Bialystok somehow given these women a shot from the Fountain of Youth and removed forty years' worth of accretions? But wait. Here was the possibility of another weapon that I could use in my relentless quest.

Like stealth aircraft, rail guns, and submarines with miniscule radar silhouettes, this love of dancing that these women listed as a favorite pastime could be used as a most potent romantic device. I also realized that although I was not privy to the biographies written by male members of online dating services, few men would list social dancing as one of their chief interests.

Wow. Not only was I a bona fide member of "The Survival of the Fittest Brotherhood," but I had also, during the course of the last forty years, innocently acquired quite a useful social skill—I could dance! While not a Fred Astaire or Gene Kelly, twenty years ago I did quite a good swing, cha cha, tango, rhumba, waltz, meringue, and fox trot. How I developed this skill bears telling.

When first I arrived in town as a new, young doc, the hospitals I was associated with had twice-yearly balls and fundraisers complete with full orchestras and professionally laid floating dance floors. When the musicians started to play, the table where my wife and I were seated would suddenly empty. The other physicians, most of them twenty or thirty years my senior, would suddenly jump up and hit the floor—not running, but dancing. Amazingly, they could do it all. They looked great in their tuxedos, and some also wore these funny flat shoes. As they spun around the dance floor effortlessly, my wife and I remained seated in stark isolation. I noticed the chill and the hostile looks I received when I told my wife I could not dance.

On my birthday, approximately one week later, I received a certificate from the local Fred Astaire franchisee announcing that I was the proud recipient of a gift of ten lessons. And so it started. Every Tuesday evening at eight, the babysitter arrived and my wife whisked me off to the studio. Despite my early protestations, things were not that grim.

I was teamed up with a gorgeous twenty-something and pulled around the dance floor. I also discovered that dancing, while not rocket science, is a skill not too difficult to acquire. On the dance floor, no one paid much attention to the man; most eyes were fixed on the woman. The ten lessons went by quickly, and my wife and I decided to continue. Numerous reasons prompted us. We were able to get out of the house sans children, we were learning a skill, I had the opportunity to hold, press close to, and fantasize with a number of nubile young women, and, most interesting of all, during the 1960s, gay people were still, for the large part, dancing in the closet.

At times when I was instructed in intricate steps, a male partner danced the steps of the woman. I was terrified that a patient, friend, or—worse yet—a relative would see what I was up to through the large plate glass window of the studio.

The male instructors were most charming, articulate, and well dressed. They were knowledgeable and could speak on topics such as cooking, fashion, antiques, furniture, decorating, and theater arts.

Our abilities continued to grow, the dance fees were now in the budget, and we were told that it was time for us to do a showcase—whatever that was. Every so often the Astaire franchises in New Jersey would hold a competition ballroom dance at one of the local hotels. Guest dancers and instructors would be brought in, dinner would be served, and the home studios would demonstrate their new students' ability. Different awards would be presented to the more accomplished neophytes. Who could turn down such an offer? To be alone on the dance floor, the spotlight on us, the full orchestra playing our requested music, and all the professionals evaluating us? It sounded great.

There was, however, one caveat. The proper clothing was required. For the male partner, this was not too difficult. I merely needed a tuxedo, which I already possessed, and a special pair of dancing shoes that were really just very light-weight loafers with kidskin soles for gliding effortlessly while performing certain steps.

Things were markedly different for the female partners. A dance dress had to be purchased and fitted. As I recall, this consisted of a full skirt that would billow out during certain steps and enhance a most attractive feminine figure. On it were sewn all kinds of sparkly things that would catch the floodlights and twinkle.

This item was not to be found in Macy's or the Gap, but could be acquired in a small shop run by a former dancer named Felix. Felix worked out of a second-floor walkup on Eighth Avenue in Manhattan. We were advised not to be disturbed by certain idiosyncrasies that Felix might display.

Dutifully, both of us appeared on the second floor, knocked, and were admitted into a large room. The walls were festooned with dance dresses, exotic female underwear—some without crotches—tops with holes in strategic places, and countless things that I identified as custom-made G-strings, both male and female. They all appeared to be works in progress.

Felix himself was a gentleman of about fifty and a bit overweight. He had some facial makeup and glided when he walked. He knew we were coming. Before we could see the dresses he had ready to show us, he insisted that we have tea with him first. We sat at a crowded table covered with sewing paraphernalia, sequins, and a large scrapbook of eight-by-eleven color photos.

The album was largely filled with photographs of a stunningly beautiful blond woman, dressed in various items. Some of the photos portrayed her in dance dresses, long gowns, stripper attire, and the aforementioned underwear not sold at Sears.

"Well, what do you think?" asked Felix after we had reviewed all the photos.

"She's a most beautiful woman," I said, "and I really like the outfits." Felix started to squirm and turned red; looking immensely pleased, he said, "It's me!"

In due course, after several fittings, the dress was ready, and the effect on my wife was breathtaking. I could not believe that I would soon be dancing with such a lovely, sensuous woman.

The evening of the competition, a large number was pinned to my back, the orchestra struck up "The Blue Tango," and we were off. The result was not a first prize, but a very acceptable bronze third place.

All of this was twenty years ago and, with my wife's illness and passing, this skill was completely forgotten. The question remained: Was dancing like swimming or riding a bike? Does it, if once mastered, stay with you forever?

At the rate I was socializing, I believed that I would soon find out.

CHAPTER 21:

Establishing a New Reality

After dating and speaking at length with the twelve women I met through online dating sites, I would like to discuss what I have learned.

First, all of these twelve women were pleasant and articulate; there was not a homicidal maniac among them. No concealed ice picks materialized from handbags. The women were all physically attractive. There was no excess weight, blue-white hairdos, or orthopedic shoes. When escorted into upscale restaurants, they attracted admirable glances from other patrons, as did I, when I flashed my new pinky ring.

My dates were far better dressed than most of the other females who were mainly clad in blouses and jeans or shorts, complete with sandals. The women I went out with had all recently visited the beauty salon and had attractive hairstyles and makeup. They looked and acted as if this date was a very important event. At the table, they did not speak with their mouths full, and they did not get noisy as the wine bottle emptied.

I, however, often spoke with my mouth full, and I became quite raucous after my allotment of wine.

Conversation, for the most part, flowed free and easy. Most of these women had had at least one not-too-pleasant experience with an online dating service-sponsored male. One woman expressed a desire to "graduate" from the online dating universe. Some offered to split the check, others did not. As an old-fashioned kind of guy who would soon be eating cat food, I insisted on paying.

All of the women were employed, almost all in full-time jobs. Among the occupations were psychiatrists, psychologists, neurobiochemists, attorneys, an art gallery owner, an anthropologist, the owner of a legal recruiting business, and a woman in charge of a merchandising firm. Most of these women had at least a bachelor's degree. Incomes listed on the dating site were in excess of $100,000 per year. They were equally divided between widows and divorcees. At this writing, I still continue to date four of these women.

At no time did I experience any rejection, and the dreaded online-dating migraine never appeared. My experience so far has been uniformly positive. Were it not for online dating, I never would have met any of these people.

People, especially seniors contemplating online dating, should realize that such dating is not entirely a benign experience. Aside from the obvious dangers posed by homicidal maniacs, financial predators, those with overt mental conditions, and date-site members with unrealistic expectations of future relationships, there exists a group of individuals, both male and female, who may present an unpleasant dating experience. These individuals, may, in the course of dating, present problems that range from an unpleasant encounter to severe emotional trauma for the unsuspecting neophyte senior dater.

The overwhelming majority of members in our senior demographic are probably not well versed in the art and science of dating. Most of us have not dated regularly and are unfamiliar with the mood swings that may occur when dates are successful or unsuccessful. We have probably been out of the dating scene for decades and now suddenly find ourselves in this emotional maelstrom of dating.

Many of us have entered this new online dating world after suffering the catastrophes of spousal loss or wrenching divorce. Now alone, we suffer the consequences of involuntarily being single again. The spouse we love is gone, our lives have been irrevocably changed, and we are forced to establish a new, unwanted reality. We are well aware that this new existence will never in any degree be what once we had and lost.

There is a normal instinct in us to try to fill the void in our lives. Unfortunately, once we've been through spousal loss and the subsequent emotional stress, our decision-making may not be as logical as it once was. We are determined both consciously and subconsciously to seek a remedy for this unpleasant situation in which we now find ourselves.

What better way is there for us to attempt to fill part of this void of spousal loss than by trying to find someone to replace what has been taken away? We wear our heart on our sleeves; we overlook character traits in those we date that are obvious to others. Should we meet someone who may be only marginally suitable for us, we may frantically pursue that individual because losing him or her and returning to the state of being alone is far more painful. We are sitting ducks for those who seek to take advantage of our fragile and inexperienced emotional state.

Through no fault of their own, male and female members may beguile us and cater to the unrealistic fantasies we have woven about finding someone who may replace the terrible void in our lives. These people are not evil or even uncaring.

They simply have their own problems and are really not interested in establishing a relationship that may lead to commitment. Their lives are likewise lonely and they relish the thought of dating on a regular basis with as many different people as possible. They are, for the most part, not interested in long-term relationships and are certainly not prepared for a monogamous situation. If one asks, as I did, "What are you interested in?" the answer is usually a single word: "fun." On some online dating sites, these people are known as "serial daters." It is important to recognize these types of members and not become part of their dating universe if you are looking for a new partner.

We, in the majority of the senior demographic, likewise seek to have fun on a date; however, we seek much more. Yet, what we desire may be unrealistic for the most part. Perhaps we have become ensnared in our fantasies. What we seek in addition to fun is a replacement, at least in small measure, for what we have lost. Unpleasant as it may be, we have to realize that this is a common finding in our age group and must be accepted as such.

Should we be fortunate enough to find a new significant other, we have to realize that this is a completely different individual who will not be at all like the person we have lost. We have started to establish a new reality, and this applies to all of the spheres of our lives. This new person we were fortunately able to meet is not a replacement or clone and never will be. If we want to continue on this new road of meeting and forming a relationship with another, we must cast off these unrealistic thoughts of filling a void and deal with the myriad fantasies that may have developed.

Online dating will present many individuals to choose from. With luck, one or two of these people may be suitable.

We must not move precipitously. Aside from careful evaluation of the prospective significant other, we must likewise search ourselves. We must be certain we are not so wrapped up in our own desires and fantasies that our decision-making is impaired and dating becomes a painful emotional experience.

CHAPTER 22:

A Singular Point of View

The majority of the women I dated and spoke with at length appeared to have common goals for the relationships they sought. Interestingly, these goals tended to differ from those articulated by the male partner involved in the date.

As previously mentioned, sexual intimacy is one of the chief reasons men look for and seek out a new relationship with a woman. This did not appear to be the case for women. When asked about possible intimacy in a new relationship, the women were more circumspect and usually replied with some variation of, "If it's meant to happen, it will," or "If true, deep feelings developed, this facet of the relationship will take care of itself."

The chief reason for these women seeking online relationships with men appeared to be for the amelioration of loneliness. The women I met were certainly not living a solitary existence, nor were they devoid of friends and family. Nearly all lived in the same geographic area as their children and grandchildren. Many of them had moved from different parts of the country to be closer to their family after the death of their spouses or termination of their marriages by separation or divorce.

Despite these strong family ties, close long-term girlfriends, and busy lives involving golf, tennis, and especially bridge, they all admitted to being lonely. Many voiced dissatisfaction with returning to an empty house or apartment after the work-day or the above-listed activities.

"The house is empty and silent," they noted. "There is no one to sit down to dinner with, no one to watch television with, and no one to share a bed with."

I asked carefully what they expected a new male friend or a potential long-term relationship with a man to provide. The answers seemed to vary. Some of the women were quite reluctant to share their living arrangements with a new man and wanted to be cautious about inviting anyone into such an intimate portion of their lives. I believe this reflected in some degree the unsavory experiences most of these woman had encountered with dates provided by online dating services.

These women wanted a relationship to develop slowly, knowing that this would give them a chance to really get to know the new partner. If emotions were to deepen, a long-term affectionate relationship could be a reality.

In the beginning, they wanted the new man to be caring, sensitive to their feelings, not given to fabrication, and—most of all—non-threatening. The women, at least the ones I had dated, were quite social. They had family support systems, and, for the most part, were still employed or had the financial ability to support themselves.

From my point of view, it was difficult to fully understand what they seemed to miss and what they were looking for. I think they essentially missed the *human touch and presence* of a male partner. I do not mean this in a carnal way, but in the sense of the genetic longings, which eventually result in the pairing off of men and women.

"How nice it would be to come home to someone who would give me a kiss or a hug, or simply replace a burned-out light bulb too high for me to reach. I just want someone to talk to, touch on the arm, or smile at," one woman said.

These women had had these experiences before with mates who were now gone. They realized what they were missing. Despite family, friends, and outside activities, an important part of their lives seemed empty.

The women would go through the demeaning experience of trying to market themselves to strangers for the chance of finding a male with whom their longings and deepest personal and emotional needs could be achieved.

It should come as no surprise to find that men and women have different expectations, goals, and emotional responses to online dating.

During the extended time in which I have been an active member of online dating sites, I have spoken with several male friends who are likewise involved in this online dating experience. The consensus among us is that this is a new technologically efficient way of meeting women. We, as a group, tend to view online dating for what it is. At times, we will meet women who appeal to us; hopefully, we likewise will appeal to them. We want the dates to be mutually positive, and we remain open to any long-range developments. We always hope for immediate positive results (*intimacy*), but are prepared to see what may happen.

The numerous pros and cons involved in online dating are probably different for each individual. On the whole, though, we men tend to view the experience as not too serious an endeavor. Most of us would not get too emotionally upset over minor irritations. I do not think many of us would become distressed or distraught should things not work out the way we wish them to.

I do believe, however, that the women members of online dating services view the experience through a different lens. After numerous e-mails, telephone calls, and face-to-face meetings with women members, I came to realize that there is a definite gender difference in how men and women view and handle the online dating universe.

Women, especially those who list marriage as their primary reason for becoming a member of an online dating service, are deadly serious. For them, this is not a dating game. They have laid it out, writ large, for all to see. Marriage is a serious business, and the steps leading to it are not to be taken lightly. We men have to be aware of this, and in our own minds we must determine whether a woman we are interested in desires a relationship that may culminate in marriage.

The woman seeking a potential partner for marriage will scour every word of what the prospective date has written in his biography. These women will recognize obvious fabrications and hyperbole instantly, and the relationship will never leave the e-mail stage. The man's name and phone numbers will be subjected to extensive online searches, and all the results will be checked and evaluated. If facts, as revealed by the Internet, do not correlate with dating-site biographies, the nascent relationship will be quickly terminated. Outright lies about age, occupation, marital status, income, or social and educational position will be viewed by these women as especially heinous.

Should the male member somehow manage to pass all of these FBI, NSC, and CIA background checks, the next hurdle will arise. This is the dreaded initial telephone call. Particular attention will be paid to timbre of voice, hesitations to questions, and catch phrases such as *it's hard to explain...I used to...in the past...to the best of my knowledge...I was young and immature*...and *I had total amnesia.*

Certain questions will be asked directly and indirectly: *Why did the marriage break up? How many times have you been married? Do you still see or talk with your wife? Do you have a relationship with your children? What is your financial status? How is your health?* The answers to all of these questions will help these husband-searching women determine whether this man wants a *nurse* or a *purse*. Depending on the initial answers given by the male, many other questions will follow.

In the same way that I would advise someone how to deal with an IRS agent, I can only offer one piece of advice that seems appropriate: Be truthful to the point of night sweats. No matter how small and how inconsequential the falsehood may appear to you, it will be ferreted out. And it will come back to devour you.

Assume, by some stroke of luck, that you have passed the telephone inquisition and are not about to be burned at the stake. Be very careful about setting up the potential date. An experience of my own will illustrate.

Although the woman I was speaking to did not appear to be one of those seeking a husband, but merely a date with a terrific guy (i.e., myself), I casually commented that I would telephone her before the scheduled date to reconfirm. Being a new bachelor, I assumed that the morning or afternoon of the previously scheduled meeting would be time enough to call. Actually I wondered whether a call was even necessary.

Upon opening my e-mail that morning, I discovered a caustic note from the female member saying, "You had promised to reconfirm, you did not reconfirm, you did not do what you had promised to do, so other plans had been made," and on and on. Being a glutton for punishment, I telephoned the avenging woman and was informed of my caddish and oafish behavior.

Ah, well, I reasoned. *It's better to find out now how despicable I am now then after I had paid for the main course.*

CHAPTER 23:

That Old Devil, Sex

I was now actively involved in e-mailing, telephoning, and dating women whom I had met as a member of several online dating sites. During this short span of time, I had socialized with more women than I had while in my twenties. In reality, life had not changed that much. I was still lonely; I missed my spouse, and I really did not know how dating myriads of women would change anything.

What was I searching for? Was it someone to fill a void that could not really be filled? Just what did I expect online dating to do for me? Was it supposed to search out women who would enable me to enjoy a torrid love affair? Would it find me a superb cook who would prepare sumptuous meals or a playmate who would join me on trips and other social events?

Upon reflection, it was all of the above. The dating site had not failed. The problem appeared to be my own immaturity and unrealistic expectations.

I now realized that after meeting and speaking with all of these women, the one thing that all of us had in common was loneliness and the overwhelming desire to do something about it. After I understood that, I became aware that the approach used to solve this unpleasant life situation was vastly different between the genders.

The men, I realized, were far less able to care for themselves than the women. They were less social, did not have the circle of close friends that women had, and they were largely inept at coping with the domestic chores of cooking, cleaning, and general housekeeping. This fact of my new life became especially evident as I kept on losing buttons and continued looking in vain for the Buttoneer gizmo that I had seen advertised on late-night television.

Then the epiphany hit. The main difference in gender approach to online dating was like everything else affecting men and women. It was the old devil, *sex*, or (to be more precise), the lack thereof. I speak now only from my own experience. The average male in his sixties or seventies, in reasonably good health, considers virility and intimacy to be of paramount importance. In our era, the difficulties of accomplishing this goal in a physiologic sense have been largely alleviated with medication such as Viagra, the use of vacuum pump devices, and—most horrible of all to contemplate—penile implants.

Although most men, especially those who are members of online dating services, are quite clever and function at high intellectual levels, there exists another more primitive brain that resides in the genitalia. The bottom line is this: A large part of the dating quest for men revolves about the bedroom.

On several occasions, the women I have dated and spoken with related episodes of infantile groping, sexual innuendo, and unwanted sexual advances even on first dates. Guys, remember this kind of behavior is a sexual turnoff for women. Think more romantically and slow down.

I now move to a field in which I am less knowledgeable. What is the importance of intimacy in the female demographic in which we swim? Most men are aware that as women age, there are certain hormonal and physical changes. It is one of nature's great jokes to make this rate of change different in the sexes.

I have read several times that the development of Viagra was a disappointment to many women. They simply could not keep up with their mates, not because of lack of desire, but mainly because of physiologic difficulties, some as simple as proper position and lubrication. I am very curious about one statistic: What percentage of women in their sixties are really interested in intimacy? Is this possible lack of interest simply physical or does it represent an emotional change after the childbearing years have faded into the past? The bottom line is this: We men have never lost our interest in sex, and many of us at this advanced age are more interested than we were as teenagers.

However, I believe that the women—and this is only my personal opinion—have a much less intense desire. So, guys, what do we do about it? One answer lies in realizing that intimacy is not the whole picture. We crave kindness, companionship, the alleviation of our terrible loneliness, and the joy of just having a loving woman around. The spark is still there. Hopefully, with proper nurturing and behavior, it will soon burst forth into a raging fire. I will also tell you that, according to my sources, a treatment similar in its action to Viagra will soon receive FDA approval and will be marketed to the female population. Guys, be careful what you wish for. It's probably going to come true.

CHAPTER 24:

I Found Someone; Now What?

Dating among sixty- and seventy-year-olds obviously differs from the type of dating we did when we were much younger. We are more fixed in our ways, and our parameters of what we desire in a relationship are different.

The time frame in which our dating is conducted is different now, as well. We no longer have the unbelievably long future of fifty or more years ahead of us. For most of us seeking a significant other, our time frame may be only one or, at most, two decades. This means that time is of the essence.

Forget about long engagements, spats that prolong the course of establishing a relationship, and unrealistic expectations we want the future partner to meet. If we are truly serious about finding one with whom to share the rest of our lives, we must reset our goals. We are no longer seventeen years old, and we have no need to learn the rules of male-female social relations.

If we have the good fortune to meet one of the opposite sex and are able to establish a relationship with that person, a situation that will serve to make both parties happy, definite positive action must be taken in a timely and forceful manner.

We must not be overly critical in our choice of potential partners. Nobody is perfect.

Most of us have been married before and now find ourselves in an unwanted single status caused by the death of a spouse or perhaps an unexpected divorce. Our new partner, if we are lucky enough to meet one, will be different from the one we had. He or she will not have the vibrancy and beauty of youth, and we will not have an unlimited time frame ahead of us. If good fortune allows us to meet another love, we must realize that this is a tremendous gift. Seize it with both hands and make it work. Not everyone is given this second chapter in life.

Try to move courtship along at a more rapid pace. If the person you have met appears to be someone in whom you will find joy, companionship, and all of the other benefits not available to singles, it is incumbent to act expeditiously.

Never compare your new love to what you once had. It will never be the same. The past is past; one must look to the future. You will never forget your first love. It is my personal belief that your departed spouse will relish the fact that you may have found another human who can provide some modicum of joy and meaning, and can take you out of the prolonged mourning and grief that have occupied your thoughts and actions since the passing of your spouse or the horrors of a divorce.

When you are with the new love who makes you happy and whole, never dwell on the life you had with your first love. This is unfair and hurtful to your new partner. This person knows that you were married before, were deeply in love, and that things will never be the same as they once were. Concentrate on the present and what you hope will happen in the future.

Put away all those photographs of your previous spouse. This is no time for a grief or guilt attack. You will never forget your first love. Avoid phrases like, "My spouse and I used to do this..." or "I remember my spouse liked..." Learn to think in the present tense. Make the conscious choice to live in the present and for future. Do not cling to the past, perhaps feeling sorry for yourself.

There is no rush to push your new relationship to the apotheosis of marriage. Stay close to each other, spend as much time with each other as possible, give thought to moving in together. If both parties desire marriage, it will come. If one partner desires marriage to such a degree that it will make a vast difference, think about it. You may not feel that marriage is important, but if no strong reasons are found for not marrying, be a good partner and go all the way. You may be surprised to find out that this is one of the best decisions you have made.

As the relationship deepens, certain changes and lifestyles will emerge as you get to know each other. Both of you most probably will have children and grandchildren. Women, probably more than men, value these close family ties and will want their new companions to join them in these family activities. Be overly receptive to this. It is a true sign of affection and represents significant progress in the relationship. You are now part of an extended family.

Learn to relate and, hopefully, be accepted by these people as a new family member. As a rule, they will be happy with the new relationship you have established with their parent or grandparent. They are aware of how lonely their relation was before meeting you; now, hopefully, this person is a changed, joyful individual because of you. Women, being more nurturing and family oriented, will establish a seamless relationship with your children and grandchildren. Your children and grandchildren, in turn, will be overjoyed that grandpa has found someone else to pester besides them.

Small things are important. If you are a confirmed "chili head" and relish jalapeños and habanero chilies, do not insist on only frequenting Mexican restaurants if your new partner prefers delicate tea sandwiches with the crust cut off. Learn to compromise. Even better yet, do more of what your partner prefers. It will pay dividends. Go antiquing with her; maybe she will go to a Mets game with you.

And now we come to the important part, especially for us men. Accept the following as fact: Women in their sixties and seventies are not as interested in sexual relations as men in the same age group. What is even worse, now we men have that little blue pill, which probably still horrifies many women.

The good news is that women in our demographic are still fond of and capable of enjoying good sex if it is presented in a loving and considerate manner. Accept as another fact that women of any age appreciate touching, kissing, caresses, lying close together in bed, and holding hands. The affectionate stroke and complimentary words and phrases imply love; caring and desirability are an integral part of their being. We guys are more bottom-line people. Women are not programmed to think this way.

Remember the old days, guys. There is an art to getting that impossible dream fulfilled. Think flowers, candles, dim lights, and lots of appropriate words and phrases. Above all, recognize that the object of your somewhat carnal desires is not twenty years old. There are physiologic issues to be considered. We guys are lucky. We take the pill if needed, unzip, and we're ready to go. If necessary, we can do it while standing on our heads, in cars, airplanes, telephone booths (if you can find one), or, in reality, anywhere.

The women in our demographic are not interested in all of this male agility. There are lubrication issues and pain issues; there may be arthritis of hips, knees, and pelvis. With patience, positioning, and perhaps medical advice, most of these potential problems can be lessened.

Realize that if a significant relationship has occurred with the help of online dating, this is only the beginning. You are now involved with another person, and the former state of loneliness and perhaps lack of true interest in life lies behind you. Both of you have been given a second chance at romance. If you're lucky, you have found a loving partner with whom you can share the joys of being alive.

CHAPTER 25:

Impossible Dream Dangers

E ven though we male members of online dating sites are usually above average in intelligence, looks, and suaveness (in my opinion), we now have to deal with two rather unpleasant aspects of the online dating universe.

I refer to erectile dysfunction and sexually transmitted diseases.

These are two facts of life that we folks in our demographic are forced to consider. We seniors are rapidly catching up to teenagers in our incidence of sexually transmitted diseases. I will offer more about this potential horror later.

There is a reason why the drugs used to treat erectile dysfunction are among the most widely used prescriptions and why over twenty million men in the United States depend regularly on them. As previously noted, intimacy is one of the chief reasons that both men and women become members of online dating sites. I am speaking about romantic intimacy, which usually appears as part of a deepening relationship. I am not referring to "junk sex," which has nothing to do with serious online dating activity.

Certain physiologic changes occur as men and women age. Among these are diminutions of the requisite sexual hormones, thickening and narrowing of blood vessels, and the effect of various medical conditions and the pharmacologic agents used to treat them. Diabetes, prostate surgery, and significant numbers of drugs used to treat various maladies found in the senior group interfere with the achievement of normal erection.

Men, in particular, perhaps due to atavistic macho feelings may hesitate to begin a relationship which will, in all probability, lead to sexual intercourse. The thought of being unable to achieve or maintain erection at the critical time is a great worry. It is important for women to understand how devastating this can be to a male who previously had absolutely no difficulty in sexual functioning. (Am I talking about myself?)

Due to the miracle of modern pharmacologic research, a solution has been found to help most men with this problem. It is amusing to think of all the effort and money that has gone into the development of this drug when the need for medications to treat cancer, dementia, and other maladies of our demographic are shunted to second place. As the ads say, "Guys, get a checkup to make sure you are not going to drop dead if things go well with an online date." This can be embarrassing to your partner and most inconsiderate behavior on your part.

Keep the little blue pill in your wallet next to the previously described round object. Take it an hour before, try to stay awake, and all should be well. If you are one of the lucky ones, you may get the four-hour erection, which, according to my urologist friend, is pure advertising hyperbole. Neither he nor any of his colleagues has ever encountered it!

I would next like to speak about the problem of sexually transmitted disease. I recently watched an elderly late-night comedian. He had some good lines about sexually transmitted diseases (STDs) but said that he had no fear of AIDS. This disease, he said, required at least ten to fifteen years to kill you, so for once he was happy to be in his seventies. He was not funny and also wrong; one can die a lot sooner.

So what does one do when a relationship has deepened to the point that both partners are ready to achieve the impossible dream? Is this the right time to turn on the lights, hop out of bed, and search frantically for the requisite note? We men have a time constraint if we have taken the blue pill. What if our chosen woman is unable to produce the certificate? (And I don't mean a birth certificate!)

As embarrassing as this may be, you are now both mature (hopefully, not *too* mature) adults who were savvy enough to use computer technology to find each other. We must believe in the germ theory of disease, have heard of Koch's four postulates, and realize that bacteria, viruses, fungi, and certain insects are only too happy to be on the lookout for a new dining experience. While most of these conditions are treatable, they can be unpleasant at best and markedly painful and even fatal at worst.

As a retired physician, I would suggest that all members of online dating sites visit their physicians and have the requisite examinations and lab work done to make sure they do not harbor any of the described *nasties*. Your physician will be only too happy to provide you with a dated statement indicating that you are in good health and not a relative of Typhoid Mary. Keep this get-out-of-jail card in your wallet and, if you are lucky enough to have multiple impossible dreams fulfilled, update it frequently.

Men and women alike should feel no embarrassment in asking to see potential sexual partners' certificates. While this action may not be foolproof, it will go a long way in relieving anxiety and will even encourage the loving intimacy that we humans so desperately crave.

CHAPTER 26:

A Computer Match Is Found

During the past six months I have been swept up in the maelstrom of online dating. I have spoken to, flirted with, and dated more women than I did during the thirty years prior to my marriage. This has been an ongoing learning experience. I have finally decided what I was searching for and what the technological marvels of online dating would do for me.

I originally began this quest because of unremitting loneliness after the death of my wife of forty-two years. I felt lost, did not enjoy living alone, and just missed the touch and presence of a woman. To me, online dating seemed a way to fulfill my juvenile notions of torrid love affairs intermingled with visions of suave social forays with numerous attractive, fun-loving, and wealthy women. Some of my immature desires actually came true during the past six months; many did not.

I now had an active social life. Finding dates and meeting interesting women for good times was no problem. The demographics were such that an unattached, reasonably active man in my age group was a rarity. Most of the vibrant, handsome, sexy males in my age group, including the ones who kicked sand into my face at the beach during my earlier years, were now safely underground. I was the rare survivor and greatly enjoyed this status.

Why was I still not content? My nights and weekends were spent in a social whirl as active as I desired them to be. I was, however, still lonely in the midst of a crowd. I had enough insight to realize that I was searching for a new first love to replace what I had lost. Rationally, I was aware that this was not possible. What was *was*. Any future relationship would have to begin at the starting point of meeting, then perhaps falling in love, and then progressing to that level where a man and woman gradually meld and, in a way, become one. I now knew that I was ready for this type of relationship. The notion of the impossible dream was in the background, but it would be fulfilled when and if this new type of relationship deepened.

I decided to continue with online dating for another three months. I did enjoy the daily computer fishing for new women and the excitement of opening my e-mail—pulling up the line and seeing what was on the end.

Shortly after renewing my membership at one particularly active site, Kismet arrived. I received a pleasant e-mail from Dee, a clinical psychologist, residing in a town about ten miles away. I wrote back, explaining that since I was forced to stop driving, I saw no way of getting together and starting a relationship with her. I thanked her for her kind words and wished her the best of luck in her own quest. This was not the first time I had composed such a response. Usually the woman accepted it, and any nascent affair ended before it began. This time was different.

I soon received an e-mail from Dee saying she enjoyed driving and would be happy to meet me on my home turf. There was genuine feeling in her response, and we scheduled dinner at Mario's. Dee was a most pleasant and attractive woman, not yet sixty-five, with a psychologist's ability to meet and interact with people and make them feel at ease. I had, in the course of the past six months, dated several mental health professionals. My biography seemed to attract women in this profession. I do not know why this should be so.

Dee and I had a terrific evening. The food was particularly good, the wine flowed, and the conversation never ceased, even with our mouths full. We both appeared to be completely at ease with each other, and I came away with the feeling that I had known this woman most of my life. As usual, I extended an invitation to Dee to see my red leather furniture and—*mirabile dictu!*—she accepted. We had a nightcap in my apartment and spoke until the wee hours of the morning. I did not push the impossible-dream scenario, but we exchanged passionate kisses as she left. (The next day was a working day for her, and she had to arise at 6:00 a.m.)

Our relationship deepened during the ensuing weeks. We were totally at ease with each other; we enjoyed the same activities, food, wine, and social functions. Dee had no children and was only too happy to meet my dysfunctional family. Over the course of the next few months, she met most of my family and friends; I, likewise, met hers. Not one of the people she was introduced to and the ones I met in turn had anything negative to say. The only one who appeared to eye me suspiciously was her cat, Calley. This relationship with the feline has improved to the point where the unimpressed animal will now meet my gaze and not hiss.

My loneliness has disappeared. I still continue to think of the great love I had and still have for my departed Pat. Dee and I speak about her frequently, and Dee's ability to accept and understand my feelings for my departed wife is perhaps one of the chief reasons I have fallen in love for a second time. I never expected this to happen, but it did. It is my opinion that we humans have the ability to adapt. Because of our mortality, one partner of a transcendent marriage will die first and leave the other behind. I wish this were not so, but it is part of the human condition. We are, however, endowed with the capacity to begin again, fall in love again, and enjoy this wonderful life we have been given.

In closing this narrative, I wish you, my readers, the best fortune in your quest for a significant other. That person is out there. Technology will help you; however, you must never give up. I do speak from experience.

EPILOGUE:

A Metaphor

Among the recent theories concerning the time-space continuum is the idea that time is not a constant. Its nature varies based on the angle and position from where it is viewed. It may speed up, slow down, and even flow backward.

It was one of those bright, unbelievably beautiful spring days in the flower garden. The air was quiet, save for the buzzing of honeybees and a chorus of birdcall. Seated in a chair amidst the flowers sat a young man, somewhat incongruously clad in a bright yellow shirt, light-colored jeans, and baseball cap.

For no apparent reason, a three-inch golden-orange monarch butterfly decided the young man was a perfect flower. The insect circled erratically and alighted numerous times on his shirt and cap. It displayed no fear, but instead insisted on finding the expected nectar. At this point, time appeared to vanish.

The beauty of the day, the magnificence of the butterfly, and the metaphor it represented overwhelmed the man.

The time frame of this experience of apotheosis may have been measured in minutes or perhaps in forty-two years.

The seasons changed. Was it the hint of a cold wind? Perhaps. Or was it really the passage of time, signifying the end of an ethereal moment? I know not, but the monarch, through no decision of its own, circled one more time and flew off, perhaps to start its incredible journey to northern Mexico, where these magnificent creatures winter, or perhaps to a more distant place in time and space.

It took the man, no longer young, a period of perhaps three years to again enter the same garden and sit in the same chair, where the magnificent insect discovered him once more. Was this the same insect that played forty-two years ago? I think not. A new butterfly had found him. The magical moment had returned. I like to think that it was a gift from the butterfly that had departed three years ago. The new insect was not the same as the old. It was more yellow in color, smaller, and not as audacious as the first one. The not-so-young man quickly realized its beauty, affection, and ability to transform the mundane into the transcendent.

My dear friends, there is joy and happiness to be found at the correct time in the future. I believe that if we will it, we can all sit in that flower garden. The monarchs will circle. They may alight on us and be a messenger from that first departed butterfly. When it happens, be receptive.

6633122R00077

Made in the USA
San Bernardino, CA
12 December 2013